THE ROAD TO ANYWHERE

Peter Pinney escaped the boredom of school to join the Australian Army in 1941, serving as a commando in the New Guinea campaign and later on Bouganville. After the war he spent fifteen years travelling Asia, Africa, Europe and the Americas on a shoestring, working in subsistence jobs when possible, avoiding French colonies when he could, sometimes on the wrong side of the law, occasionally rich, often hungry, and always writing. He wrote *Dust on My Shoes* in Calcutta, *Who Wanders Alone* in Zanzibar, and *Anywhere but Here* in London.

In Central America, he ferried whisky and cigarettes from the Panama Free Zone to adjacent republics, lost his schooner in a gale, and became editor of a small Caribbean weekly. When he released distressed animals from a Martinique zoo, the French deported him in the direction of Australia where he wrote *The Lawless and the Lotus, Restless Men,* and *To Catch a Crocodile.* He spent five years craying in Torres Strait, then married the cook, Estelle Runcie, in Daru, Papua New Guinea, sold the boat and wrote *Too Many Spears* with Estelle. Between 1988 and 1992 UQP published his jungle warfare trilogy *The Barbarians, The Glass Cannon* and *The Devil's Garden.*

Peter Pinney died in October 1992.

Sydney-based travel writer and photographer John Borthwick is the author of five guide books to Australia and one to Tahiti. He has published many articles on travel, culture and destinations in various Australian and Asian publications. He holds a PhD in travel writing from Wollongong University.

Borthwick's work as a travel writer, on documentary films and as an adventure travel leader has taken him to many odd parts of the world. A collection of his travel stories, *The Circumference of the Knowable World,* will be published by UQP.

Other books by Peter Pinney

THE ROAD
TO ANYWHERE

The Travel Writings of
PETER PINNEY

Selected by John Borthwick

University of Queensland Press

First published 1993 by University of Queensland Press
Box 42, St Lucia, Queensland 4067 Australia

Typeset by University of Queensland Press
Printed in Australia by McPherson's Printing Group, Victoria

Distributed in the USA and Canada by
International Specialized Book Services, Inc.,
5804 N.E. Hassalo Street, Portland, Oregon 97213-3640

Cataloguing in Publication Data
National Library of Australia

Pinney, Peter, 1922–1992.
    The road to anywhere: the travel writings of Peter Pinney.

    1. Voyages and travels. I. Borthwick, John. II. Title.

910.4

ISBN 0 7022 2552 5

CONTENTS

INTRODUCTION

THE MAN WHOSE HEART LAY ON THE FAR HORIZON

"In a cobbled lane with a pompous name there was a well appointed tavern ..." From Mozambique to Martinique and almost everywhere in between, Peter Patrick Pinney (1922–1992) was always finding the door to adventure's tavern slightly ajar. He rarely failed to push it open and step across its fateful threshold.

"Nobody ever lived their life all the way up except bull-fighters", opined one of Hemingway's characters. As far as I can tell Peter Pinney never fought a bull, though he did do battle with a spectrum of foes, from Japanese marines in New Guinea to sour-mouthed French bureaucrats in at least a dozen colonies. Probably more than anyone else I have read — and certainly anyone I have met — Peter Pinney lived his life "all the way up". Yet he was not an aggressive or self-aggrandising man. The foppish machismo of a bullfighter would probably have struck him as vapid, and a cruelly unequal match, to boot. In fact, Pinney thought of himself as "just an ordinary, unremarkable sort of bloke — which often was very helpful in certain tight situations".

This "ordinary, unremarkable sort of bloke" made a true profession of travelling — not as a tourist or explorer, but as a modern picaro, an in-it-up-to-the-neck Zen nomad. His 1948 to 1950 overland journey (described in *Dust on My Shoes*) from Greece to India and then Burma pioneered the route which a later generation of '60 and '70s hippy trippers turned into the Dope Trail pilgrimage. Whereas most of them became stalled in the eye of a chillum in Goa or Pokhara, Pinney and his friend Marchand trekked on, illegally, across Assam and into head-hunter country in upper Burma. There they were told, "No white man has come through those mountains since the British forces in 'forty-five...and they took an easier route than you.''

His books are replete with frontiers: some physical, some political, and many bureaucratic (he regarded "bickering with the Law" as "a natural corollary of travelling"). But journeying for Pinney was not just the storming of obscure borders or the accumulation of anecdotes as "next book" fodder. Instead, it was his work — both physical and intellectual — and his pages carry self-reflective passages where, often in conversation with some more sedentary soul, he ponders the traveller's philosophical conundrum: the slings, arrows and ecstasies of the peripatetic life, versus the surgical drip certainties of hearth and taxes. A fat but unhappy baker somewhere on the Niger River warns him "...no man can be happy if his heart lies in another place, apart from him". To which Pinney considers the possibility that: "Unhappy, then, is the man whose heart lies on the far horizon, and always moves ahead." And keeps on moving.

Peter Pinney's continuous moving ahead commenced while he was at a Sydney boarding school. He learned to "ride the rattlers" during his holidays and saw much of the east coast from freight trains. By the time he had matriculated, his senses of both adventure and irreverence were sufficiently well honed that all he wanted (or was suited) to do was travel. But that was 1941, and travel then meant becoming a "dollar-a-day tourist" in the Australian Army in the Middle East.

"I was firstly a traveller, then a writer," said Pinney. "If I hadn't travelled I wouldn't have been moved to write." With Army travel he started a life-long discipline of diary-keeping, which in the Army was of course illegal; the censors captured his tiny, secret book, written in miniscule script and "filigreed" it with a razor. Undeterred, Pinney continued recording; when transferred to a jungle commando unit in New Guinea (and later in Bougainville), the cat and mouse game of preserving his diary from prying official eyes continued. On this occasion Pinney was the victor, a success which later made possible (and became one of the plot lines of) his trilogy about that campaign, based on his diary notes.

As a writer Pinney was an untutored natural. Riding freight trains, crawling through Japanese lines, and living on your wits from Salonika to the Slave River may merit a double PhD from the university of life, but it is no particular apprenticeship in the art and crafting of prose. Yet, from the beginning his style was lyrical, clear and witty, with a novelist's feel for dialogue, character and plot. Of writing his first book *Dust on My Shoes* (at age 28) he noted:

> There seemed to be a great deal of work involved; and it nearly didn't get written at all. I was in Calcutta, and I was broke, my last few rupees having been stolen as I was standing in a tram. But having dealt me several unkind blows, Fate allowed me to make the acquaintance of half a dozen airline pilots — American, English, Australian — who proved anxious to have someone look after their house. In my spare time I could write. I had no idea how to write a book. My only feedback was when one of the pilots picked up a typed page and read a few paras, laughed with friendly derision and handed it back.
>
> But I stuck at it. I wrote 180,000 words and sent the manuscript to Angus & Robertson. They said they would accept it — "but cut out 60,000 words". If someone takes you to the top of a high mountain and says, "All these lands I will give you, if you cut your wife in half'", what do you do? So I cut out 60,000 words, whole sheaves of pages, adding a line here and there for continuity. And it became a best-seller, despite that derisive laughter.

For some twenty years (and through six civil wars), Peter Pinney lived to travel. He did not travel in order to live by his writings. His peregrinations through Asia, Africa, Europe, the Americas, the Pacific, New Guinea and Australia became the grist of six travel books and one novel. During the 1960s and 1970s he skippered a cray boat in Torres Strait and along with his wife Estelle Runcie, wrote *Too Many Spears*, a dramatised biography of Frank Jardine, Government Resident on Cape York in the wild 1860s. By the 1980s he and Estelle had settled in Brisbane, where he wrote television scripts (including *The Sullivans*, *Carson's Law*, *Flying Doctors*) and finally, a trilogy of novels (*The Barbarians*, *The Glass Cannon* and *The Devils' Garden*) dealing with his jungle war experiences against the Japanese (which he had also covered in a very early novel, *The Road in The Wilderness*). Twelve books, six civil wars and at least ten passports are not a bad innings for a travel writer.

Not long before he died I had the privilege of meeting Peter

Pinney. I first came across *Dust on My Shoes* in 1968; having all but lifted the print from its pages — such was my youthful enthusiasm to absorb it all — I then went on to read everything else of his that I could find. Credit, blame or thanks are due to him for having presented vagabondage to me as a perfectly worthwhile career option. Thus I travelled, and later became a travel writer. Having the chance to finally meet a "hero" in the flesh is to run the risk of encountering but a shadow — or a parody — of what one has imagined. Peter, on the contrary, turned out to be all the humorous, compassionate and fair dinkum things that his pen had suggested — and much more. I think he was a bit of a "living national treasure" (if not a "global treasure"). Those people I know who have read his travel books are all a little envious of his living, for he did it so fully — indeed "all the way up".

When I was asked to select an anthology of Pinney's best travel writings, the enduring question became (and remains): "How can I leave out *that* bit?" In fact, I have left out whole books. It was soon evident that the quartet of books which cover his extended absence from Australia, from 1947 to 1962, formed an extended narrative. Episodes from other travels would be jarring intrusions in this suite of works; thus, fine passages from Pinney's rambles in Australia (*Restless Men*) and his time with George Craig, crocodile hunter in PNG (*To Catch a Crocodile*) have been omitted. In turn, from the four books of his major journey, I also had to reluctantly discard precious episodes, such as him peddling whisky and baked-beans in Beirut, stealing moonshine on St Kitts, playing Marlon Brando's double in *Mutiny on the Bounty* — and much more. I hope that the excerpts which follow do justice to the scope of Pinney's wit, spirit and writing, and lead the reader back to the source of their richness, his original works.

Finally, many thanks are due to Estelle Runcie Pinney for her generous contributions and advice in all phases of the preparation of this collection.

JOHN BORTHWICK
SYDNEY, 1993

DUST ON MY SHOES

PETER PINNEY's first book, *Dust on My Shoes*, is the account of an overland journey which he made (between September 1948 and November 1950) from Greece to Burma, via Turkey, Syria, Lebanon, Iraq, Iran, Afghanistan, Pakistan and India. This route — in turns, toxic, terrifying and hilarious — was later known to Western trippers and drop-outs as the Overland Route or the Dope Trail. For the penniless Pinney and his sometime travelling companion, Robert Marchand, however, it was a continuous frontier of extreme experiences, all the way out to and including death.

GREECE

"I am just travelling. Some people like to grow crops, others to make music, or sit in small shops, like your father, selling pots. I am unsuccessful in all the things which I enjoy most, except the one thing which I find best of all: and that is travelling. To pass through a new country is something very dear to my heart."

"But why Turkey?" said Georgios.

"Why Greece? Because I have not been there before."

"Then you must be a rich man. It is expensive, travelling."

"No, I am not rich. Sometimes I have money, and sometimes not. One becomes lean sometimes, and then fat. One becomes hungry sometimes, but never starves."

He gazed at me uncertainly, and said. "You are a strange man. I should find nothing to enjoy in such a life. No security, no future. What will you do when you are old? You will have no money."

"But I am growing richer daily, and when I am old, if indeed I live to be old, I shall be rich beyond measure. I shall have such a harvest of memories as shall warm my heart until I die."

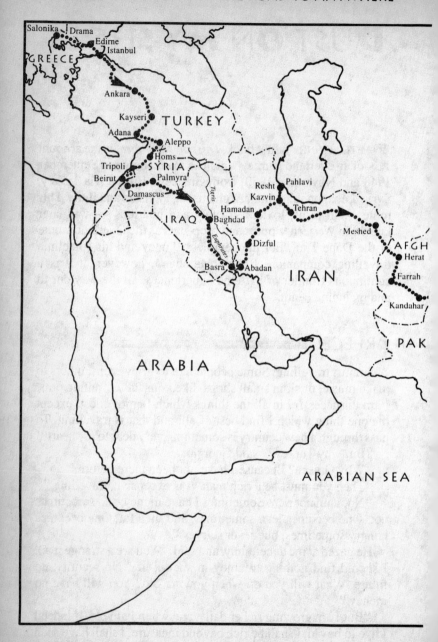

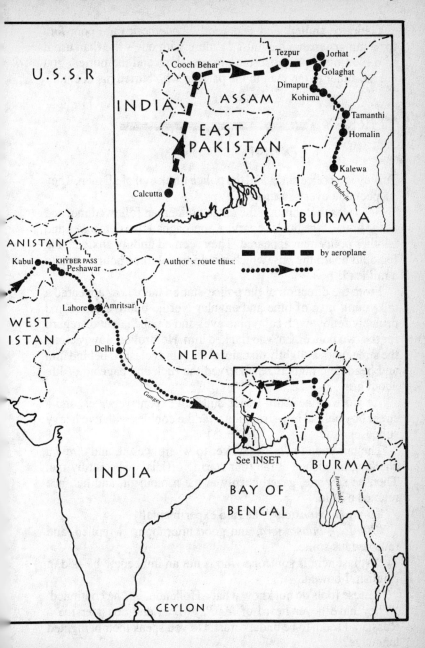

U.S.S.R

INDIA   ASSAM

Cooch Behar   Tezpur   Jorhat
                          Golaghat
                Dimapur
                Kohima

EAST
PAKISTAN   Tamanthi
                          Homalin

Calcutta   Kalewa

                          Chindwin

                BURMA

ANISTAN

Kabul   KHYBER PASS
          Peshawar   Author's route thus: — — —   by aeroplane
                                                    •••••••►••••

          Lahore   Amritsar
WEST
ISTAN
          Delhi   NEPAL

                    Ganges   BURMA

                          See INSET

INDIA   BAY OF
                          BENGAL   Irrawaddy

          CEYLON

Georgios smiled, and said gently, "Memories are poor fare for a hungry man. One must do more with one's life than use it as a blotting-paper, absorbing impressions and memories. You are a brother to the man in the parable who buried his talent."

TURKEY ═══════════════

EDIRNE

Turkey is a police state, and the police think evil of all men. They suspect that every stranger is a spy.

So it was that through the day a policeman followed me, and as the hour of the bus's departure approached two detectives and another policeman appeared. They seemed unduly anxious that I should board the bus, which would travel three hours south to a railhead.

From the direction of the police-station there now appeared a tall young man of lithe and angular Nordic build; a blond and princely fellow with calm blue eyes and a nonchalant disregard for the two policemen who flanked him. He strolled slowly along the street with a slightly disdainful air, hands clasped behind him and head held high as he observed the ruck and pageant of life about him.

He wore a fine Palm Beach suit and expensive shoes, and a street boy behind him struggled over the cobbles with two heavy suitcases.

The tall young man came over to where we sat, and threw a challenging glance at the four staring officials who sat by me. Then he saw me, gazed keenly at me a moment, and his face relaxed a little.

"*Bonjour, monsieur,*" he said experimentally.

"*Bonjour, buona sera,* and good afternoon," I replied, and returned his smile.

"At last here is someone who is not an imbecile," he said in English. I bowed.

"These fools do not know what a Hollander is," he continued. "They have never heard of *les Pays-Bas*, and consider me a Russian. I seem to be under arrest. Do you speak their benighted language?"

"No, I arrived only yesterday, from Greece."

"And I this morning, from Bulgaria. But is there not a war in Greece?"

"And is there not an Iron Curtain about Bulgaria?"

We regarded each other with interest. I wondered who and what he was, this self-possessed and scornful traveller. The bus was ready to leave, and now the police — there were no less than six of them — began to grow restless.

"It is time to go," said one. "This bus is about to leave."

The traveller noted their uneasiness and smiled. "*Alors*, I suppose I had best go; the sooner I get to Istanbul the better. You are not coming?"

"I am; but not on this bus. It is expensive, being first class; in a half-hour's time the post bus will be leaving, and I am told the fare is only one-quarter of the other."

"So? Then I shall travel with you, on the cheap bus."

The stranger's name was Robert Marchand, and the world was his native land. He was an adventurer of Dutch and French origin, an engineer by profession. To live was his ambition, and he viewed his misadventures with the objective and analytical detachment he used in solving chess problems.

"It was difficult getting the Balkan visas," he admitted. "The Bulgars won't give you a visa unless you get the Slav one. And the Slavs won't play ball unless you already have a Bulgar one. So I had to cheat, played one against the other, and gained both in the end."

His passage through the Balkans had been marked by less incident than one might have expected.

"Where," I asked, "are you going, after Istanbul? Or will you stay there?"

"I have a visa for Egypt; probably I'll go overland, through Syria. And you?"

"Perhaps I shall take a ship to some other country. Italy, maybe; it is a beautiful country, and I have seen no city to equal Rome. But Egypt — it was ever a land of morons and sycophants, and now that they have gained independence they're showing their teeth to foreigners. You will be robbed if you go there, and worse."

He laughed with a light heart.

"Robbed of what? When I arrive in Istanbul I shall walk out of the station without a sou in my pocket. My Turkish visa had gone stale and I had to use my last few shillings to bribe the frontier guards to let me cross. I shall have to sell my clothes to pay my passage to Egypt. My reason for going there is no better than that I have never been there before; and doubtless, as you suggest, I shall be glad to leave. Do you play chess?"

"More or less."

"Good; I have a set here. How true was the sage who said,

'Tis all a Chequer-board of Nights and Days.
Where Destiny with Men for Pieces plays.'

"I have never met a Tasmanian before; and on the north-west frontier of Turkey is as strange a place to meet one as I can think of."

∧∧∧∧∧∧

ISTANBUL

Istanbul is an ancient and many-tongued metropolis, once said to be the wickedest city in the world.

It is a storied city with a turbulent history, an old and wrinkled grand-dame with a young and lively heart of commercial offices and stores, of clanging trams and streamlined limousines. The Galata Bridge reaches across the waters of the Golden Horn from the mosques and alleys of old Stamboul to Galata, to the banks and cinemas, the docks, to the grand parks and elegant hotels of Beyoglu.

Marchand and I stood on the Galata Bridge and watched the trams and trucks hurry by, the near-naked porters saddled with great loads, the melon-vendors and cigarette boys, the beggars and the cosmopolitan throng who passed by with no surcease to traffic and noise. He had left his two suitcases at the station.

At one end of the bridge rose a great domed mosque amid a rabble of tawdry shops, cheap restaurants and tenements; at the other end were the docks, the waterfront dives, and the trunk thoroughfare which curled left and up the slope.

"Where shall we live?" queried the debonair Marchand. "By the docks, or by the mosque?"

"It is pleasant to have the choice."

There were small hotels on either side.

"If we seek a hotel by the docks," he reasoned, "they will think us to be seamen, and either rich or destitute. And one will be accosted by all manner of sharpsters in the streets."

"Then let us live by the mosque. There is a vegetable and fruit market on that side where one can buy melons. Cheaply, too."

Walking back towards the station, we found a melancholy little dive tucked up an alley where cans of garbage overflowed their trash upon the flagstones, and here we inquired if there were rooms.

"Yes, I 'ave rooms," leered the snag-toothed witch in the dank and ill-lit hall.

"How much do you charge?"

"What do you want? — long time, or short time?"

"Well, let us say a week."

The witch was astonished.

"A week?" she shrilled, and cackled derisively. "No man can stay at it a week. What you think you are? Horses?"

A blowsy girl appeared in a doorway, her limbs fat and dimpled, clad only in a flimsy open blouse and a brief skirt, Marchand nudged me.

"Wrong house," he muttered, and chuckled softly.

ᨺᨺᨺᨺ

ADANA

Alea had a provocative figure, Spanish features, and a French education. Her features were piquantly Latin, delicately shaped to support an infectious smile; the smooth alabaster of her skin was tinted with the natural bloom of youth, and further enhanced by the French-style fringe of her blue-black hair, which swept low upon her forehead. She moved with a stirring feline grace, her slim figure shown to advantage in a white satin blouse and red satin trousers caught at the ankles, and when she spoke her voice was a soft caress, her English flawless.

One could not but wonder what brought her to such an infamous place.

On an upstairs balcony she sat down at a table opposite me and sent an urchin to bring coffee and an iced melon.

She asked me who I was and where I came from, and I told her.

"But you are not a seaman? That is what I thought you were, though this is not a port." She was noting my worn clothes, the sloping heels of my old boots, the travel-stained leather lumber-jacket, the stout but uncreased corduroy trousers.

"Do you like seamen?" I asked, and she laughed lightly.

"No, you are not a seaman, or you would have bruised me before speaking. And you have little money, I can see. Ah well, there have been times when I had nothing; when the Germans left Istanbul at the end of the war, work was hard to get. For a year I worked in the Manhattan Cabaret on Galata, then I went to Izmir. But that sort of life is no good for a girl — one has to drink too much — so two weeks ago I came here."

"Hard life?"

"Hard enough, though I'm a sort of special reserve as yet. Only the old or ugly ones have to work hard, for they are neither fussy nor expensive; but it is tiring, and one does not rise till nearly midday. I have heard that they are going to close these places down, and I guess it'll be a good thing if they do, but I don't want to go back to cabaret."

The coffee came, and a melon which we sliced and ate with honey. Over us was a canopy of grapevine, and now that the clouds had gone the sky crowded with stars, and strong moon-light poured through the leaves and dappled the table and floor, casting light and shadow on Alea's lovely face.

The air smelt sweet and clean after the rain, and the cloying scent of ripe grapes mingled pleasantly with the steam from the rich coffee.

Her hands were small and shapely, and the sweet curves of her mouth denied her loose philosophy.

"You are very beautiful."

She smiled. "That is because my father was a Spaniard, and my mother a Circassian."

"Spain is a land of lovely women."

"And the Circassians? You have not heard of them? Then let me tell you that among the mountains between the Black Sea and the Caspian you will find the most beautiful women of the world."

"Many nations claim that heritage."

"Circassia used to supply the Turkish slave-market with the most lovely women to be found, and many of them became the wives of grandees and of the palace courtiers. Their fame spread into Europe; and rightly was one of the reasons why the Russians seized our land a century ago. In Circassia itself the marriage custom is such that the suitor must buy the lady of his choice from her father, and then pursue and catch her on horseback; and, if the lady is not willing, that is not always an easy thing."

"Here is a bad thing," I said, "I have no horse."

She dimpled. "Neither have I. Where will you sleep to-night?"

"I know a hotel where the lice are big enough to bound about; which is convenient, for large lice are easily caught."

"Not if they are so athletic. I know of one where the lice are small, but for a few kurus you can have a washed sheet."

"In my place are seven beds in one room, so that one will not be lonely in the night; and the window has no glass, so the ventilation is good."

"The place I know is better, for there is a key to lock the door and even a mirror on the wall. True, there is only one bed, but it has two pillows."

Commotion broke out in the street below; police were making a raid. By this time the street had filled with strolling adventurers, and queues were forming in front of all the doors.

From the balcony we could see eight white-uniformed men of the Turkish police moving about, six plain-clothes men and four army provosts. They were thoroughly searching all the men this end of the street, and the entrance had been cordoned off. Outside the opposite door about twenty men were formed up in a jostling line.

"They make a raid sometimes," explained Alea, "to search the men for weapons and dope. Hashish. There is a great deal of hemp produced in these parts, and though it is illegal many of the girls smoke it."

"But why do they search for weapons?"

"Because sometimes a girl comes in here and she has a lover

outside who becomes jealous, and tries to kill her. It happens, believe me. They search everyone coming through the gate."

"You girls are allowed out?"

"Yes, we have passes. Only licensed girls with a doctor's clearance can enter this street. But come, let us sit on the sofa. Would you like some wine?"

Later I went downstairs, and after changing she slipped down past the whore-mumma and joined me outside the gates. Through the restive bazaar we walked towards the river, her laughter tinkling merrily in the dark secretive squalor of the dim back streets; and where a great and ancient arched stone bridge spanned the main river we turned to the right along a group of coffee houses.

The Yildiz Hotel was as all small Turkish hotels are: mean and faded, the narrow crooked corridors echoing with the shuffling and cautious panting of a multitude of unimportant people, some happy, some melancholy, some diseased and others frightened, all of them poor. The stench of their passage poured out from the greasy latrine, which was a ragged hole in the concrete floor above the river-bank. The worn bare wood, the dirty walls and broken locks, the sagging beds and clumsily wrought furniture were mute testimony of a certain way of life.

The proprietor was the oldest man in the world.

He was as thin as a blade and his eyes were rat-bright in a peaked and sallow face, as if long ago he had forsaken the sun and tempered his body to the narrow confines of the inn. Without speaking he led the way to a room as far as possible from the latrine and giving on to the river. He turned the pillows on the bed to the cleaner side and addressed Alea.

"One lira."

"Yes. Coffee."

At the window we sat sipping at more coffee, rich with brown froth, and eating cakes of honey and ground pistachio nuts which she had brought. In the room below men were playing backgammon with noisy clatter, drinking tea from glasses, and the eternal coffee.

"If one wish were granted you," asked Alea, "what would you desire?" Her lustrous eyes were fixed upon the mosque and slender minarets illumined in the soft moon-glow at the other end of the bridge.

"What else should I desire?"

Her eyes were troubled. "No, I don't mean this; it is only temporary, and the mornings are always so bleak with hard reality. What would you demand of life? Riches, or some rare ability? A kingdom? Perhaps an island paradise?"

"I once knew a hermit who lived in the face of a cliff, and he had none of these things. But he was a happy man, and he told me that he had one thing which few men ever had for long; and that was peace of mind. It seems that if you have this thing, then others are not necessary or even desirable."

"Well, I haven't got that. My mind is like a bee in a winter garden, restless, hungry for something better than this. I am always afraid of meeting someone I know, or of dying before I have bought and burnt sufficient candles to receive remission for my sins; for you see, I am a Christian. Sometimes I have a dream: I am in a cathedral, and about to die. But no matter how many candles I buy, God sits implacable on His throne and gazes right past me. Candles and more candles come, till the church is filled and there is not room for any more; then the church is alight and there is fire all about me. . . . It frightens me. Above all other things, I would like a child."

I smiled. "That should not be difficult.."

"But it is. There are many things. . . . Oh, to be free as you, to travel, to see other lands! I would like to go to America. Is it true that marriage there is a two-year contract?"

"Sometimes it is longer. Are you interested in marriage?"

"What girl is not? But the Turks. . . . You see, I am part Spanish, and though there are no better soldiers than the Turks they are poor lovers; they are revolting, and there is something in me which rebels against them. They are ill-mannered and ungentle."

She put her hand in mine, and I caressed her smooth fingers. For a time she was quiet, then she looked up with peace in her eyes and smiled.

"It is nice, just to be here with you."

Through the night the hotel room became too hot, so we walked across the bridge and wandered among the orange groves on the other side till we found a clean place at the river's edge, and here we swam by moonlight in the pebbled shallows.

The first colour of dawn was in the sky when I awoke. Alea was asleep on the grass beside me. For a long time I looked down at her, then rose and washed and walked off into the dawning.

∿∿∿∿∿

In the dusk I swung aboard a train.

There was a fat Egyptian in an empty compartment who spoke French, and when he saw me swaying along the corridor he glanced quickly at my clothes and invited me in. On one finger was a large diamond ring which he played with unceasingly.

"Well, sit down, sit down. Cigarette? I was just wondering if I should have to travel without company all the way to Aleppo?"

"I am going to Gaziantep, on the Syrian border, and perhaps to Aleppo." At Gaziantep I might have to leave the train to avoid ticket-collectors; such money as remained was insignificant.

"Will you join me in a drink?" He had produced a flask of cognac, and reached for the two glasses in the rack. His neck was unsightly with folds of fat, the nails of his stubby fingers were discoloured with nicotine; the heavy shadow of ungrown whiskers tinted his slack jowls with blue, and bushy black brows stood out starkly in the unhealthy grey pallor of the remainder of his face.

He regarded me with interest as he proffered the cognac. His hand was fat and flaccid, and brushed against my own. "You have been to Aleppo before?" he enquired.

"No."

"Ah, it is a fascinating place, and there are such gay girls." He laughed and smiled slyly at me. "You like the girls, eh?"

"Sometimes. How far is it to Gaziantep?"

He glanced at his watch.

"Shortly. Perhaps twenty minutes. But you will not get off at Gaziantep, surely? There is nothing there, nothing at all. Just a police barracks, and the station. Is it that you lack a ticket? Or perhaps you have no papers, and must hide? Very well, I shall help you. I shall buy you a ticket and if necessary shall even help you hide. Come, another drink."

"If I have a ticket, it will not be necessary to hide, and I will willingly go with you to Aleppo."

He glanced at me quickly, and put his hand on mine. "Aha! I think you and I will get along well together, is it not? You shall lack nothing while you are with me. That is good, eh?" His tongue raked his moist, fleshy lips.

And so it was that when the train hissed and ground to a stop at the last station before the Turkish-Syrian border, a ticket to Aleppo was bought for me. An unending stream of people tramped up and down the corridor outside; sometimes the door would be wrenched open and slammed shut again. Outside the windows one could see that soldiers were stationed along the side of the train watching the windows.

All the doors were locked, and from either end the customs and immigration officers began working systematically towards the centre. The immigration came first, two inspectors attended by police. The door was flung violently open and they crowded in.

"Passports."

The Egyptian handed them his thin green book and immediately became involved in some abstruse argument which entailed a small bribe. My book was scrutinized but accepted without question, and adding the passports to their collection the officers continued to the next compartment. My companion licked his lips, and smiled.

"They are difficult people the Turks. Very suspicious people. You are American? Or perhaps German? I did not catch your name."

The reply was interrupted by the arrival of the currency experts. They peered into the Gyp's wallet, which was comfortably fat, but they did not search either of us.

One of them caught the Egyptian's hand and examined the diamond ring, but two liras were pressed into his hand and he forgot what he had seen. After we had signed papers they left.

An hour passed before the customs came to our carriage. They had with them a powerful flaring acetylene lantern which threw grotesque shadows along the corridor. Bags and baskets were emptied remorsely on the floor, the contents of suitcases were scattered out on rugs, thermos flasks were tapped and tasted, and paper bags and parcels were fair prey for the police and customs alike.

Again we were not troubled unduly. The Egyptian had turned his diamond ring around so that it appeared to be a plain gold one.

Time passed. Outside, the yard lights and the moon shone on lines of motionless goods trucks and the patient guards, and distant sounds of activity came thinly through the night. A man was led away from the train to one of the station buildings, followed by a protesting family trailing improbable impedimenta.

The immigration officers appeared again and returned our passports, complete with exit endorsements. A whistle shrieked and the train drew out.

The Egyptian was becoming drunk and increasingly familiar. His hints were neither subtle nor pleasant, and the thought came to me that I did not like Egyptians. For the nth time he breathed wetly in my face and squeezed my hand, but at that moment the ticket-collector appeared. The Gyp belched mildly and produced two tickets; the collector looked at them and passed on.

"You see, I am looking after you. Eh? What do you say?" He put his hand on my leg and tried to kiss my face. I rose to my feet and hit him twice, once on either side of the jaw, and he slumped. Selecting the bigger bills from his wallet I poured the rest of the cognac over his clothing and left the flask on the seat, and quit the train as we were entering Aleppo early in the morning.

SYRIA ▬▬▬▬▬▬▬▬▬▬▬▬

ALEPPO

"German? No. There is no German here."

"Possibly not German; Russian, maybe?"

"Of good height, and fair? A Polish Jew, then?"

Parts of the conversation seeped leadenly through my consciousness. A German. A Jew. Fair. I had slept well and would presently go out to eat.

"... last night. This morning he was seen near here. We must search the hotel."

The sûreté! So my Egyptian had resented the little joke, and here were the police. It was time to go.

The windows were barred. If I went out of the door they would surely see me, a fair-haired man among a race of dark headed Arabs. Already they were opening doors and peering inside rooms; but there was a chance.

Picking up my shoes I moved quietly to the door and pulled it well ajar, open as far as the hinges would permit, and steadied it with a chair. Mounting the chair I climbed cautiously onto the top of the door and edged my way up the wall. Standing thus on top, my hands pressed against the ceiling, I might well escape detection.

"He is not here," protested the proprietor. "Always I make people register, and take the names of foreigners as well as the numbers of their passports. Of course," he added worriedly as they approached the open door, "sometimes there comes one who sneaks in and sleeps without paying."

But they did not see me, they just glanced in at the empty room and walked on. Immediately I climbed down, and still with my shoes in one hand went quietly out into the street and made my way into the teeming bazaar. "Have you sore feet then?" asked a voice from a bric-à-brac stall. "This is holy ground," I muttered, and hurried on.

▌IRAQ ═══════════════════

BAGHDAD

"You have no right to be in this country. And none of your damned insolence!" hissed the police chief.

"We were informed," I stated levelly, "that the visas —"

"Arrgh! Be quiet!" he rasped furiously, his voice edged with hysteria; and in that moment we saw that he was a dangerous man, an uncontrollable man. "I tell you that you have no right here. You must go. Do you hear? At once. I want none of your damn lies. It is of no use for you to pretend."

This was too much. The harm had been done, our position could scarcely be worse. Marchand leant forward and pounded one large fist on the shining desk so that the inkwell rattled and the pencils jumped.

"Listen to me, you *verdampt* Arab!" he snapped. "You just don't call me a liar any more, understand? Two of your police told us the visas were valid for fifteen days ..."

The chief had risen to his feet and was trying to outshout him, eyes bulging, his face pale with rage. He fairly screamed in Arabic, and it sounded as if bedlam had broken loose in the office. I wondered what it felt like to be deported. Police were rushing in with cries of alarm, a lamp-shade splintered to the floor; so I added my moral support and howled fortissimo, "And if your benighted bloody country is run by such an incompetent pack of yokels that they can't read their own language —"

"To court!" screamed the chief, his voice breaking. Police had seized us by the arms. "To court! You'll go to court!"

"You know what you can do with your court!" we chorused, and were frog-marched ignominiously outside, with the out-raged chief still waving his arms and cursing us at the top of his voice.

As Marchand reflected philosophically some time later, there is a proverb which says, "Whom the gods would destroy, they first make mad."

The court was near the river, not far from C.I.D. headquarters.

Around a great flagstoned yard was a double tier of box-like rooms where the intricate cogs of the Iraqi interpretation of justice were slowly turning. In the courtyard several hundred people sat waiting or walked aimlessly about; poor people with not enough money to pay heavy bribes, luckless individuals over-awed by the bustle of activity in the rooms above, the rustle of papers and lawyers' robes, and the loud announcements and summonses by the crier.

Pilgrims from Persia were there, a favourite trick of the Iraqis being to allow them to enter the country without a visa and then to arrest them and fine them three times as much as was right, for there is little love lost between the two countries.

Jews were there, to pay exorbitant taxes, or to go to jail if they could not; Assyrians, to pay more taxes and three times as much as an Iraqi for any form of licence. And Iraqis by the score, to pay two or three dinars for such petty offences as annoying a policeman or throwing pork in a synagogue.

After various formalities we were led into a cool, dimly lit chamber where a mullah sat in state behind a carpeted desk; for in this country the religious leaders are also the judges. He was an old man, and peered short-sightedly at us through his spectacles. For a few moments he shuffled through the papers which had accumulated in our dossier, and then he piped, "Are you Christians, or are you Jews?"

"Christians," we answered.

"Case dismissed."

INDIA ===============

DELHI

"No luggage, sahib?"

"None at all."

A worried frown crinkled his brow.

"It is perhaps ... held at another hotel where you could not pay?"

I handed him one rupee, and the frown disappeared. He hurried away and returned with a bowl of water.

"Rose-water," he explained, sprinkling it about the floor and walls, "for sweet-smellingness. Every day you pay one rupee, and everything is good. And next door to you is a German guggler, with many pretty flowers in his room."

I eyed him askance. "A what?"

"A German, who is a guggler. You will meet him tonight; he speaks good English."

"When he finishes the day's guggling, no doubt. *Eh bien*, so be it. Thank you."

Krueger Sonovitch was a Yugoslavian, not a German. He was more than a juggler; he was an acrobat, chiropodist, clairvoyant, signwriter, sharpster, shoplifter, and something of a horticulturist.

Perhaps his most outstanding characteristic was that of arrant fraudulence. He was above all things a dishonest man, with a scheming brain which led him to lucrative conquests in varied fields, and cunning fingers which could enter people's pockets unperceived. Sonovitch was uncommon in that he considered, with tears in his eyes, that his own loss was greater than that of any man he robbed.

Once when he came home with some valuable trifles he emptied his pockets on to the bed and regarded the things with dismay. He stood looking down at them, a slightly built and bare-headed figure, pathetically clad in ill-fitting clothes; and with misery in his voice he said, "I am not as other men. How it must be to be light-hearted, and to know one's honour."

I wondered that he should contemplate his trophies with such lack of enthusiasm, but he was a sentimental man.

"If these were honest things, how I would treasure them." He sighed heavily, from his heart, and sniffed. "Doubtless they were highly prized by their owners, and now … They will be hating me, despising me, and even if I would, I could not return them. So many things I have stolen, and where is the profit? It is said that even he who steals the whole world gains nothing but his grave.

"My mind is haunted by the echoes of the cries of purseless women and watchless men; their pleas and threats are held prisoner within my mind, as if within a drum. I hear them at night."

The walls of his room were hung with orchids, brightly blooming, gleaming like frosted porcelain, and dribbling moisture on the floor. Some quirk of his nature made him keep these beautiful things close to him, perhaps to afford him company in those dark moments of the night and day when memories closed in on him. When I admired them he evinced no interest, but poured himself three fingers of Indian rum and drained the glass at a single draught. Soon his dismal mood vanished, and after we had each imbibed and had examined the trinkets once more he patted my shoulder and said, "Well, first acquire money, then practise virtue, eh?"

Every morning Mr Sonovitch walked through the narrow streets and the bazaars of Old Delhi to see what lovely things the day would bring him. In one hand he carried a small valise containing a powerful bar magnet. That side of the valise usually fitted with hinges was missing, so that when it stood upright on the ground the magnet was free to pick up any little thing underneath, and hold it in concealment.

In a busy side-street, we paused to admire the various articles of a barrow-man's display — a barrow divided into sections containing a wide assortment of such commonplace articles as buttons and brooches and cigarette-holders, plastic combs, and so on. The Yugoslavian held the case low over the barrow in front of him, and with simulated interest he examined this thing and that, asking the price and discussing the worth. Slight metal clicks emanated from the valise, but these were lost in the general clatter of the traffic and aroused no suspicion.

When at length we moved away he steered me to a quiet corner, there to peer into the case and examine his magnet, and lo! Providence had surely smiled on him, for attached thereto were three thimbles, a button-hook, eleven knitting needles, a pair of keys, an American screwdriver, a pair of Sheffield nail scissors, a flute, pins without number, a chromium-plated watch-chain, two teaspoons (guaranteed sterling silver), a pair of odd cuff-links, and a small surgical device for the Painless and Instant Removal of Warts, Piles, and Corns.

Sonovitch grunted, and muttered, "So, I have once more missed the handsome razor."

"But what of the odd cuff-links?"

"I have one little sack full of such cuff-links. Do you lack cuff-links?"

"Thank you, I have no cuffs."

"Ah, it is a pity."

He glanced with interest at my clothes, and appeared to be engaged in calculation.

"Your clothes are unfortunate," he admitted, "all except your shoes. They are a very fine pair of shoes. That is the only shirt you possess? Well, perhaps we can come to some arrangement."

On return to the hotel we sat on his bed and discussed a plan which he had in mind.

"You have seen these beautiful orchids?" he asked. "I am in the orchid business. I have a friend who is a pilot, and every week he brings me orchids from a certain place I will not mention, Burma side; hillmen find them cheaply and I do not pay a great deal. They are flown here from more than a thousand miles away, and I sell them for good prices."

"Indians would not be very interested in them, would they?"

"Indians? There is nothing I would sell to Indians, except maybe rat-poison hidden in chocolates. No; there are still many Europeans in Delhi among the consulates and big firms, and to them you will sell easily. It is a good job, no?"

"It sounds promising."

"But I am busy with acrobatics and things, I must always be practising and supervising, so I do not have a good chance to go out and find nice prices. I think you maybe can do this for me, and get the commission, eh? I put you in pretty clothes so that you look handsome and respectable, and away you go and visit the big sahibs and memsahibs — the ladies are always interested in well-dressed young men — and you sell the orchids. There is a good market ... while I make sure there is always a supply, I also make sure the demand is constant."

He pulled a box from under his bed, and showed me a syringe.

"This is my little baby," he crooned. "With this I make the orchids to die. I put arsenic into them; I inject just a drop into the roots. It makes them to bloom quickly, but in two, three months the plant dies ... and the customers come along wanting more ... So you see, there is always a demand for orchids."

For a period of one month life was conditioned by the sale of orchids. They were not always easy to sell, but business progressed and the delicate slipper blooms adorned the reception offices of the Imperial Hotel and the Taj, and various restaurants in Connaught Place: tall and slender blooms of *Paphiopedilum*, chocolate and green, were brought in lots by the staff of the French Embassy, and more sparingly by the Chinese Ambassador's staff, and honey-yellow and green blooms of *Paphiopedilum villosum* were raffled by the office forces at the British High Commissioner's. Orchids, orchids everywhere: all slowly dying.

From four-anna snacks of chupatti and dahl in wretched taverns I graduated to one-rupee meals in cafes with tablecloths and electric fans, and finally reached the stage when I wore hand-painted Dali ties and silk shirts to dine and wine regularly in the air-conditioned palaces of Connaught Place.

Sometimes I wondered where Marchand might be, and if he would come to Delhi. Had he, indeed, come through Afghanistan, or was he still in Persia?

It was towards the end of the month of sales that Sonovitch came to my room bearing a paper, exclaiming excitedly that he had found Marchand.

"See! He is in the papers! He has been writing like a newsman, even his photo is here. I can tell you he will be a famous man in Delhi."

Marchand was in Lahore.

There had been a mild earthquake there, and a church steeple had narrowly missed falling on his head. Now here he was in all the splendour of page three in the *Amrita Patrika*.

WORLD TRAVELLER COMES TO INDIA.

MR MARCHAND REACHES LAHORE.

One evening as I was returning to the hotel, intending to make Krueger Sonovitch a gift of a bottle of fine chablis that I had purchased, I perceived from a distance that two policemen lounged in the cafe adjacent to the hotel entrance, and that two others strode off down the street bearing the hapless Sonovitch between them. His two performing monkeys scampered along behind. He was bare-headed and his clothes were in disarray; he was speaking rapidly to the two escorts, no doubt trying to bribe them, but they dragged him to a police van and rudely thrust him inside.

Possibly his two monkeys, which he had painstakingly trained for many months, had been observed in one of their frequent raids on open windows. They would run up fire-escapes or drain-pipes till they found an open window, and unless disturbed would steal anything which appealed to them: hairbrushes, magazines, mirrors, and sometimes more valuable articles such as pieces of jewellery and cameras.

So I left such trifles as were in my room and went away to the house of Rajindra Nath, who was also a very good friend, though honest.

Marchand arrived, riding triumphantly down Queensway on

a bicycle, with a new hat and a bright red neckerchief fluttering from his throat.

We made acquaintance with the pilot who had ferried orchids to Sonovitch, and went our way.

ASSAM ====================

Laruri was the last village in the administered territory. Across the foaming torrent in the gorge below was headhunting country. The good track ended. Ahead of us towered the ten thousand-foot range which was the Burmese frontier; the border ran along the top. Laruri was perched high on the side of a steep valley through which the Ti-ho river ran, and occupied a series of strategic knolls surrounded by stout palisades of wooden stakes.

Like other villages, Laruri was split in two by the coming of Christianity so our welcome was double-barrelled; but invariably we stayed with the heathens, for the Christians gave us no beer.

Marchand dumped his pack on the ground, and sank gratefully onto a smooth log.

"There's Burma," he said, gazing at the sombre bulk of Tsekhung and Mount Saramati. Saramati was twelve and a half thousand feet. "It is a big mountain. What are we going to do when we get to the other side?"

If we had known, we would not have gone. The topmost heights were hidden in banks of cloud; the whole sky was a brooding sea of dark cumulus. The rains would surely come soon.

"There's a bridge across the river." He pointed to the swirling brown waters foaming through the depths of the gorge far below, on their way south and east to the Chindwin River, in Burma. "Rain has fallen somewhere in the hills, but we can still cross. This is the last big water until we reach Burma."

We had walked off our map, so began negotiations, by signs and the few words of the language which we knew, for a guide on the morrow; but no man would agree to come with us. The villagers pointed to the east and with their long knives they tapped their limbs and throats.

"What do they mean?" asked Marchand; but their meaning was all too clear.

"They mean that the natives in those mountains will be delighted to take off our heads and cut us up. And that no one is prepared to go along with us to be similarly treated, for which one cannot blame them. Marchand, are we being damned fools? The only weapon we have with us is a meat-axe."

He pursed his lips and gazed calmly at the formidable mountain barrier ahead.

"These things always sound worse than they are," he said with nonchalance. "It has been the same all the way — you can't do this, it is impossible to do that — and here we are. I don't think we've got anything to worry about."

"Except our two skulls. It might be difficult to replace them. But I suppose now that we've walked this far, we may as well see what happens around the next corner."

The monsoons broke during the night.

Thunder rattled and boomed across the sky, the sound of the rain was like an advancing waterfall. With a flurry of wind and a restless tossing of the trees it swept down the valley and drummed loudly on the earth and vegetation and the hut roofs. The night air was filled with a fine spray, the roof leaked, puddles formed on the earthen floor, and outside in the darkness a few rotten boughs crashed to the ground.

Towards morning the rains abated to a fine drizzle.

The *gumburra* stood before us in the village compound in the dawn and tried to talk with us. We understood none of his speech, but the general idea was made lucid enough by extravagant gestures.

"If you go across the river," he was saying, "you will be killed. Your heads will be taken, possibly you will be eaten, and no one will be able to do anything about it. So it is better for you to go back to Pek, to Kohima."

When we insisted on going across he gazed a moment at the mist-shrouded wilderness ahead, made a pattern in the mud with his toe, and with the end of a stick he drew a circle about us. He then ordered two white fowls to be brought, and motioned us to step from the circle. The two fowls he put inside it, and chopped their heads off, and held them fast till their frenzy ceased and they lay motionless within the circle.

Two red fowls he gave to us, and a seer of long-grained rice.

He climbed down with us to the river, and said his smiling farewells at the entrance to the swaying cane suspension bridge. We gave him tobacco and a plastic comb; he saluted us and waved us on. We made our way carefully across the bridge, to tribal territory on the other side, wondering if we would return and what might happen if we did not.

The track was an overgrown pad a few inches wide skirting a precipice above the swollen river; a monsoonal squall hit us and we clung blindly to the cliff-face till it passed. Climbing, crawling like ants around the base of the towering Kungtsi Rock we moved over roots and stones through narrow corridors of tall dank jungle, by open grassy knolls and gloomy dripping tunnels of foliage, six hours' march to Lungphurr, the first headhunting village.

Lungphurr was heavily fortified, the palisade bristling with sharp stakes, clinging like a limpet to a steep rocky slope.

It was approachable by only one track, and three astonished guards challenged us; none had seen us approaching, since the gardens were all east of the village and we came by an unused trail from the west. We were escorted through the spike-studded entrance and the elders came out to see what had arrived; the compound was an evil-smelling mire tipped at an angle, the houses built of stacked slate with slate roofs and piled higgledy-piggledy up the slope.

The braves were well-muscled men armed with an interesting assortment of weapons; all we had was our meat-chopper, and we offered up a prayer.

From each house we passed there issued a litter of children who scampered along in our wake, the elders crowding to the doorways to stare. The skulls of dogs and birds, of pigs and bighorned water-buffalo, adorned the facades of many huts, and by their number gave some indication of the standing of the family within.

Near the chief's hut were two great hollowed hardwood logs which served as drums and were capable of transmitting messages over long distances. On a long pole by a tree sat a row of grinning human skulls, grisly with their newness; fowls pecked at the maggots which fell to the earth below. Bamboo stakes protruded from the eyes, and each head was pierced vertically by a stake which affixed it to the pole.

A group of braves came down from the upper huts and indicated that we were to take our packs and follow them up the slope to what seemed to be the village hall. The crowd watched intently as we lifted our gear and answered the summons of their king, flanked by warriors with spears.

The chief, a lean and grizzled old gentleman, grunted and motioned us to enter his hut. It was a very large and stoutly built affair with heavy beams supporting a high thatched roof. Inside it was very dark, for no light could enter the hut except from the door or through the chinks between the thick wooden planks forming the walls. Everything in the hut was a mellow brown, smoked and cured by the wood-smoke of years rising in a thin lazy stream from the glowing embers of a deathless fire. The wooden poles supporting the slate roof were liberally varnished with a black shining coat of smoke-paint; the burnished lights gleamed and glistened from pots and huge urns, from the steel blades of spears and long knives, and shimmered on the broad blade of our own chopper.

In a circular arena of stamped earth we stood at ease admiring the rippling muscles of the young braves and looking at the odd collections of carvings and weapons with what we hoped was an attitude of friendly nonchalance.

The braves and elders squatted or stood about the arena in a circle, and held council.

Questions were asked of us, and we could not answer because we knew not what they said. Even the few words we knew were useless, for the dialect here differed from that of Kohima side, but they understood where we came from and where we wished to go.

*"A Kowhira noo vorr. A Tamanthi key votuo."**

* "We come from Kohima. We go to Tamanthi."

Tamanthi was a river-station on the Chindwin, well over the border, and was known to these people for they nodded their heads vigorously and the name Tamanthi was bandied to and fro.

*"Soddu, viseh."**

We pointed in the general direction of Burma, and they understood. They chattered and bickered among themselves, the chief squatting aloof and observing us with a cold regard. Men held aloft faggots of yellow-orange pine-wood, richly charged with resin, which burnt with a generous flame. Their heavy pungent fumes mingled with the smoke of the smouldering fire and the smell of unwashed bodies.

Wise men and warriors alike felt our clothes and ran their hands over our boots, felt the fatness of the unfortunate fowl still trussed to one of the packs, and considered with mounting interest the gleaming silver meat-chopper. The chief grunted his appreciation, felt the edge, and weighed it in his hand. No doubt it was a heavy and satisfactory weapon for in-fighting, or for chopping up strangers.

We presented it to him, along with our only mirror, and he received each with a non-committal grunt.

Marchand pulled an old trick. The occasion had not been entirely unforeseen; we had thought we might meet with un-friendly people in the tribal area and had considered what we should do. He took an ordinary bottle of clear glass from a shelf, evidently a prized possession in these parts. All eyes were on him as he half filled it with water from a bamboo container, and they muttered among themselves as he squatted on the floor and drew magic patterns in the dust with one finger.

While they were watching the patterns he slipped some crys-tals of permanganate of potash, which we used to purify drinking water, into the bottle.

He held the bottle suddenly aloft and shook it vigorously. The water turned a purplish scarlet. A loud and appreciative buzz of excitement filled the hut, and the chief watched with a little awe as a purgative tablet was dropped in the water and began to effervesce.

Bubbles foamed from the bottle. The water was obviously

---

* "Tomorrow, very good."

boiling. Marchand lifted the bottle to his lips and drank, draining the bottle at a single draught, and the braves shouted and yammered among themselves. We could have sold a case of tablets on the spot. Marchand rubbed his stomach and smiled at them.

Again he half filled the bottle, handed the chief a pill and persuaded him to drop it and drink. The old man eyed the foam a trifle nervously, but honour was at stake and cautiously he tested it.

Finally he drank, then smacked his lips with relish and rubbed his flat belly as had Marchand.

The braves and elders howled their approval, and the chief's eyes glowed with triumph. He beamed gladly at us, happy that he was not belittled in front of his men, and sneered a little at his fellows with a haughty air. Here was a king indeed, who could equal this unheard of magic.

Marchand handed him a glass phial containing a dozen tablets; the chief studied them carefully and put them away in a small pouch which hung about his neck.

Beer was brought, a syrupy clear liquid with the power of raw spirit but pleasant to drink; the chief and some ten of the elders drank with us. The braves dispersed. By the light of the pine torches we squatted on rattan mats and smoked and drank. The chief was not a healthy man; his swollen spleen suggested malaria so we gave him four paludrine tablets, eating one ourselves as encouragement.

No doubt he expected more magic, for he swallowed them cautiously and held his belly tight.

Two of the elders performed a wild-eyed dance in the arena, with stabbing spears and stamping feet, moving to the primitive rhythm of a throbbing tom-tom pounded by a gleeful savage.

Marchand and I sang "The Rose of Tralee" and the chief performed one miracle after another by drinking boiling beer. He drank thirteen purgative tablets, and no doubt he was thoroughly purged and purified by the morning.

We caroused far into the night with song and laughter; we didn't mind if the world kept spinning or went straight ahead. The evening closed in a fog of disremembrance, and everyone was happy and that was all that mattered.

In the morning we had difficulty in securing a guide.

After much discussion, when we were on the point of moving off with no guide, the chief gave us his own son, Chamoo, and two young stalwarts to carry our packs: this in return for the last of our silver pieces which, as they seemed well aware, could buy wondrous things from the outside world.

Out by the spiked entrance we walked, past the three guards and along the top of a cleared garden area. The main Burma trail lay to the right, up a steep spur leading south and south-east; but Chamoo made us understand with pantomime that danger lay that way and we would go through the dread land of the Kula by a secret path he would show us.

Throughout the day we made slow and laborious eastings. It was indeed a secret way.

We descended into the depths of a ravine at the head of the Turatu Valley and groped in abysmal gloom through heavy jungle growth which had smothered the narrow trail with the passage of years, so that often the way was lost and we had to cast about.

It was hot in such thick jungle, and perspiration soon drenched our clothes, matted our hair, and trickled down our bodies to collect and squelch in our shoes. The air was foul with a dank earthen smell and the odours of decay.

In nine hours' constant climbing and hacking we covered three miles.

Lawyer vines tangled the way with a mesh of thorns, nettle-trees seared our flesh with hot rashes. Each slimed precipice of loose shale or moving rock threatened accident; we climbed up by means of vines and ingenuity, scrabbling for toe-holds and shouting advice, dodging falling stones from those above and gingerly testing each rotten ledge or hand-grip. Leeches in their thousands craned thin eager necks at the tremor and scent of our approach, sometimes gaining a hold unseen, bloating and bursting with a mess of blood inside our boots.

Tribes of monkeys stormed through the tree-tops hooting and screaming; at dusk, when the crickets were shrilling mightily and sunset was an occasional glimpse of a flushed cloud, we climbed up from the stream we were then following; climbed a hundred feet through a forest of nettle to the lair of a panther, a black and musty cavern where big pug-marks could be seen in the loose dry dust.

The five of us shared what we cooked, eating from the flat fronds of banana palms, a hot and cheering rice stew liberally seasoned with chillies and salt. They were friendly and companionable men, jungle men with jungle ways and the smell of earth and wood-smoke on their copper bodies. Tea was brewed, with the last of our sugar, and they received half.

Mists closed in and the rains poured down.

We were at the foot of the last great climb, but the mountains above were lost in a sea of greenery which enveloped us, and in the white moving banks of mist. Heavy drops rattled on the bouncing broad leaves, and fine spray drifted in on us. Marchand sat drying his boots and socks by the fire, and gazing dreamily into the coals. Dusk had fallen; the shadows were deep.

"What're we doing here, Aussie?" asked the Dutchman. "Why are we sitting by a fire in an animal's lair three stops past Buggery, listening to monsoons and wondering whether or not we'll still be alive tomorrow night?"

"You make me nervous."

"But is it getting us anywhere? Is there any object?"

I rubbed my nose, and reflected aloud, "There's Mandalay, and Rangoon ..."

But Marchand was not satisfied. He spread his hands to the blaze.

"Something drives us on, from one place to the next. Perhaps we seek something, not knowing what it is, not even realising that we seek at all."

It was a problem which I could not solve. We had travelled through Europe and across Asia to the back door of the Orient; and perhaps it was because I was tired, or ignorant, or unwilling, that I did not reply. I rolled my thin calico sheet out on the dirt and lay down, smoking my pipe and listening to the rain.

BURMA

Slithering down from the border, down the mountain slopes, we passed through heavy squalls and emerged from the rainforests to find the track becoming well defined. Our descent was swift. The farther we were by nightfall the better: the guide and coolies were uneasy and even while we moved they were listening … We were on the edge of the bad country, close to the land of the Kula.

Soon after noon we met the first sign of the headhunters.

Chamoo was leading, myself next, Marchand behind, and the two coolies bringing up the rear. Chamoo cried out in pain and collapsed on the track. Marchand yelped out a curse and doubled up. The native was groaning and holding his foot, the two bearers had thrown their packs on the ground and were glaring about them at the empty jungle, moving their spears restlessly in their hands.

"Clean through my leg, Pete. A wooden stake."

A sixteen-inch bamboo stake had passed through his leg above the ankle; a *panjyi*, a tribal boobytrap set to discourage invaders. They were sown all along the track. I was standing among them.

Chamoo's wound was the more serious, for the stake had penetrated his foot between the bones and veins, so he was tended first. Whipping open the packs I took out sulphanilamide tablets, cottonwool, and a spare shirt. The tablets were crushed to powder, the shirt torn into strips, and Chamoo's wound bandaged. *Panjyis* are usually dipped in a satanic cocktail of poisons and kill within ten minutes, so he had torn the stake from his foot and blood spurted freely between his fingers.

The carriers watched the son of the chief as he rocked back and forth softly singing to himself, the sweat running from his face. Marchand jerked the stake from his own leg with a gasp of pain; the two wounds were neat and easily bandaged, but they continued to bleed for a long time.

"Damn and blast the Kula," he cursed. "We've brought ourselves a load of strife."

"Can you keep going?"

"If I don't pass out from poison, sure. There's no use in staying here, and I'm damn' sure I'm not going back. But Chamoo — he may take a dim view of this sort of thing and return to his village."

Chamoo was shivering with shock. He expected to die. But

fortunately the rains had washed away any poison there may have been on the stakes, and neither Marchand nor Chamoo died.

"Perhaps the carriers will string along with us."

"One of them will have to stay with Chamoo; he's going to be a sick lad. And it's improbable that the other boy will go farther by himself. They've been unhappy ever since we crossed."

Chamoo grunted heavily and pointed to another stake set by the edge of the track at an angle of thirty degrees, best designed to pierce the foot of a man; there were others, a score of them in ten yards, cunningly concealed under fronds of fern or overhanging plants.

But neither of us had gauged our men correctly. We had not realised what manner of men they were. Chamoo finished examining his bandage, obviously in a lighter frame of mind since no ominous symptoms had developed, then rose to his feet and accepted a stout staff a carrier had cut for him. With a grunt and a glance at us he signalled the carriers to take up their packs, and stepping clear of the track he began to hack a passage through the jungle.

This was so slow and laborious that I went ahead along the path flushing the traps with a staff, and we proceeded at about one mile an hour. Another thousand feet we descended, and at the bottom of a great valley came to a rushing stream and a good trail which led north and south.

At intervals it was studded with bamboo stakes. We followed it across subsidiary streams and over sharp rises and slippery descents to the south, watching for any sign of the Kula. I went ahead, prepared to take off at speed should a group of head-seeking savages appear abruptly before me; for we would obviously be enemies, coming down this forbidden trail.

Chamoo was having difficulty in moving. A great balloon of semi-congealed blood had formed under the bandage, and when the rag was loosened and the flabby bladder of redness plopped to the ground he groaned and looked away. He had to be assisted up the steep pinches and shepherded with care down the other side.

One hour along the trail when I was bending low searching for the stakes, a five-foot *panjyi* almost punctured my chest. It was set to catch a man in the stomach, long, three-cornered, and very sharp.

Chamoo indicated the mountain-side and made us understand we must climb to circumvent the main village of the Kula; the Kula were near and the men were nervous.

We climbed. Chamoo was fainting periodically and Marchand was labouring, his face white and strained, but we climbed steadily for an hour.

Then, below us in the great valley, a single drum began to throb.

The ominous tattoo rolled and echoed along the hills. The braves paused, and glanced at us with apprehension, muttering among themselves.

"Kulami! Kulami."

They pointed in the direction of the drum, and we nodded. Chamoo leant against a tree and vomited tiredly. We moved off again and tried to increase our pace — and indeed the jungle was thin here and did not hinder us — but Chamoo's steps were becoming increasingly erratic and someone had to support him constantly. His foot left a thin trail of blood behind him. Blood had collected in Marchand's boot and squelched as he walked.

An hour passed.

Among the foliage below us a bird whistled. The three natives stopped dead in their tracks, and listened intently. The whistle came again, two shrill notes. The Kula had found us.

The three braves whispered excitedly among themselves, and then called out, and someone shouted from below. Chamoo sank wearily to the ground and we waited. How could we flee with two wounded men?

The chief of the Kula himself appeared, leading a patrol of six men.

He was a strapping young savage with the muscled limbs and powerful chest of a hillman; he was a magnificent specimen of manhood. But we were interested at the time in the .303 British Service rifle he carried, and in the six slim spears of his grim-faced followers.

He advanced slowly, and stood with impassive face and ready rifle while he squinted narrowly at us and observed every detail of our clothing and visible equipment. His warriors gathered about us in a semi-circle, and with one hand raised in salute Marchand and I made what we hoped was the sign of peace.

Chamoo rose unsteadily to his feet, drew himself to his full height, took his red blanket from a satchel to throw about his shoulders, and faced the chief of the Kula; Chamoo himself was the son of a chief, and would answer the questions which were to be answered.

There followed questions, disputes, and furious wrangling. Questions and accusations were barked at him, and he rallied his strength and pride to snap back replies. One felt he was not a diplomat, but one accustomed to speak his mind. The Kula's eyes flashed dangerously, Chamoo sweated and shivered with fatigue and fever. During the heat of the argument, which lasted for almost an hour, the six warriors closed in round us; our two carriers dropped their loads and fingered their own long spears.

Down below in the valley the drums kept up a monotonous tattoo.

Tenseness gradually relaxed as the chief and Chamoo talked on. Once the chief even smiled, his teeth showing strong and white, and the atmosphere became more cordial. What was being said we could not tell, but at last we were escorted to the Kula village, the very village we had wished to avoid, and found the people there assembled for defence; the men had been called in from the gardens and clustered in groups inside the stout palisade, the women peeped wide-eyed from the inner huts.

These people do not bury their dead; instead they place them in coffin-shaped containers on stilts by the village gate, where they rot. On the seventh day the head is severed, and in a farewell procession the sightless eyes stare for the last time on those places the dead one had enjoyed most. Then the head is set back in place; the flesh and worms drop to the ground and are devoured by pigs, dogs, and chickens.

Now, as we approached the village, our nostrils were assailed by the stench of putrefaction emanating from a cluster of such open graves standing by the gate.

The chief took us to a hut among the grain-houses above the village perimeter on a grassy slope, and found us fair accommodation on a bamboo platform. The wounds of the wounded were tended, pills distributed to the sick who came up from the village with rotting toes, and carrying their scabrous infants, and the chief watched with interest and approval. He was fascinated by a cheap but elaborate penknife we presented to him, and grinned hugely when Marchand affixed a safety pin through a hole in the lobe of his ear; thereafter he was undoubtedly our friend.

A fowl and eggs were presented to us, and large bamboos of beer were brought to quench our thirst and cheer us. They talked some gibbering dialect and we were speaking French, but we managed well enough and made our gratitude clear when a fine papaya and part of a dog were given us.

The rains had ceased and the mists were gone; white clouds drifted below us among the blue-green ranges, troubled cumulus shrouded the sky above; dusk drew in and we saw the rays of the sun for the first time in several days. We could see south down the valley towards the Ti-ho river, over rolling hills patched with the black of new gardens and the green of old ones, and saw the village of Yawparmi several miles distant on the other side.

Behind us, three miles distant, was the lumpy crest where we had crossed the frontier at noon.

Chamoo and the carriers were coming no farther with us, so we paid them many times the agreed rate of hire with all we could spare of clothes and trinkets, giving Chamoo half our salt and sulphanilamide, and wondered a little sadly if his foot would ever get better, or if it would rot with ulcers.

Four days' march took us to Tamanthi, through Yawparmi, Chungko, and over the Ti-ho, or Tiku, by a swinging cane bridge to Hungpea. The Kula provided us with an escort out of their country, and through friendly villages we marched over the last of the mountains and down among the foothills to the Chindwin River flats and Tamanthi.

∧∧∧∧∧∧∧

KALEWA

He had a dignified presence, this monk with whom we talked; in appearance he was not unlike Gandhi, though not so aged. His pate was shaven and shiny, he wore gold-rimmed spectacles from thin ears to lean hooked nose, and sat cross-legged with unconscious grace, his slender hands at rest upon his lap.

As we talked the sun was rising high and the mists folded their tents and stole away, shadows grew a little shorter and the dew was turning to vapour.

At length our friend Cockeye told the *punjyi* the reason which brought us to the monastery, our desire to acquire a letter of safe conduct through troublesome territory. He had heard of us from the villagers, so there had been little chance of posing as missionaries. We had told him the truth.

"It is possible," he said, "for me to give you a letter. But you must consider these points. Firstly, there are many communists along the road to Ye-u.

"Secondly, there are other, equally lawless people who would certainly rob you, if they did no worse, and they would be quite unlikely to realise the significance of any letter, even if they could read it. You would be most unwise to go."

"And chicken-hearted if we did not," said Marchand. "We intend going, but consider that a letter from you would assist us in time of trouble."

"Despite the bandits, cut-throats, and communists who would destroy you? There is a civil war. There is hate abroad such as the world seldom sees. And such misunderstanding ... My poor people follow any man whose voice is sweet."

"Despite these things, yes. True, it is a civil war; yet the night is ever fraught with devils which disappear upon inspection, and we have learnt that fences scorned are fences half crossed."

The monk considered his slim brown hands, and for a moment was lost in thought.

"It seems you have not yet travelled enough," he observed. "You claim your travels are bringing you a measure of wisdom; yet where is your common sense?"

"It is our common sense, and the wisdom of former experience, which teaches us the limit of the danger."

The other shook his head sadly, and rejoined: "I know what I know ..."

He turned to me and said, "Show me your hand. Your left hand."

I extended my hand to him, and he took it in one of his, holding it a certain angle that the lines thereon might be seen to better advantage. He perused them a while with the objective interest of a professional palmist, muttering a little, and then indicated a line leading away from the base of my third finger.

"This line," he said, "is the present indication of your fortune. It is unbroken, and that means your luck is good. Doubtless if you go to Ye-u you will arrive in safety, though possibly robbed. You should wear a golden ring on the third finger of your left hand."

He loosed my hand and took Marchand's; and it was at once clearly seen that the relevant line on his left hand was broken.

The monk frowned, and examined the hand closely through his gold-rimmed spectacles. Then he released the hand, and raising his head he regarded Marchand levelly and announced, "Your fortune is very bad. If you go ... you will not arrive, and you will not return."

The air seemed hushed just then, and the shadow of a cloud fell across the glade. There was a ring of sincerity in the *punjyi*'s voice, as if he knew only too well that he had read the portent true, and that what he had said would come to pass. A shiver trickled down my spine, and then the cloud was gone, the crickets were chirruping again, the sunlight blazed on the hillside and Marchand shrugged, half smiling.

"Fortune has never failed me yet in such matters," he stated, "and doubtless this line has been on my hand for some years. Why should it suddenly assume significance?"

The sky was patterned with flying clouds, the Chindwin was burnished with silver by the noonday sun, when Marchand and I stole out of the bungalow and down to the water's edge. No man saw us go. We had seen the canoe there among the shrubs and knew to whom it belonged; Marchand went to dicker at the hut of the owner, paid half a rupee for the afternoon's hire, and returned with two stout paddles.

He regarded the canoe with speculation.

"It's best we sit fore and aft, like they do," he commented, "and place our packs in the centre."

"The current looks fierce ..."

"No matter. We have a stout canoe, and if the Burmese can paddle across, then so can we."

The river was sweeping by at an alarming rate. The surface was troubled and broken with small whirlpools and disturbances, the waters hissed as they rippled back on themselves and surged this way and that.

"Perhaps," I observed dryly, "we should test the mettle of the river first, and become acquainted with the whims of this canoe."

He was indifferent.

"As you wish. But let us not waste too much time. The police may disapprove of our intentions."

Our packs were placed in hiding with our clothes and shoes. Clad only in shirts and underpants, we stepped with care into the nimble craft and sat at either end facing the bow, Marchand for'ard and myself aft. With a glance along the river-bank to see if we were observed we pushed out, and were caught at once in an upstream current which habitually ran along this section of the shore.

Then the vagaries of this anti-flow ceased, and we moved out into the spate of conflicting rips and rapids. The edge of the flow was flecked with a brown-white foam, and simmered with purling ripples. The craft began to slew this way and that, and it became increasingly difficult to steer.

We paddled in rhythm, Marchand and I, without straining and with due regard for balance. The canoe responded nervously to every move we made. The paddles dipped and flashed with a quiet gurgle; we kept the bow pointed upstream at an angle, but were carried diagonally downstream, out towards the boiling mill-race in the centre of the river.

The rips and cross-currents grew worse, gripping the slim craft powerfully. Turmoils of water mushroomed up and slid outwards in a circle to rustle below the surface. She bucketed through a surging storm of water shot with squalling eddies, slewed upstream and tried to ride a sudden flux of current in towards the shore.

"Make in!" I cried, and helped her turn a little farther, so that we headed inshore, again at an upstream angle. We had seen enough. We could handle the canoe well enough to sustain a reasonable chance of gaining the farther shore.

The flow of the river was bringing us down towards the level of the township.

Local whirlpools swam beneath the hull, sucking and gurgling; the cross-fire of lawless tides snapped and swirled viciously, purling about us and chopping at the hull with malevolence.

There was mischief afoot.

Overcurrents and undercurrents bullied and baited the canoe, but we made good shoreway and drew close to the first cluster of houses.

Twenty yards from shore we were still paddling vigorously, when a sudden surge of current mushroomed beneath us. The canoe lifted. The water boiled outwards from the centre, and we skidded with it sharply to starboard, thrust willy-nilly and rocking severely. But another power of mushrooming current convulsed the surface there, so that the two disturbances threw their weight upon each other and the canoe was trapped in a hissing rip of writhing waters.

A rush of brown flood stormed over the starboard side. The canoe was half filled. Marchand glanced over his shoulder, but his paddlestrokes did not falter. Even as we dipped our paddles anew, the tide surged against us once more, foaming over the side and filling us to the gunwales.

The canoe foundered, and sank beneath us.

We remained seated till the water came up to our shoulders. Then we stood, and the canoe was thrust from under us. Our shirts billowed with imprisoned air, then deflated and clung soddenly to us. We said no word. The shore was fifteen yards distant, but we could not swim to any purpose with our shirts on, so wrenched them off and let them go. The watertight rubber pouches containing our passports floated from strings about our necks.

The canoe slowly surfaced, bottom up, like a waterlogged porpoise. Marchand was swimming for the shore, but I clung to the canoe and intercepted the paddles, and looked to the shore for assistance.

A woman had seen us. She was shouting excitedly to her friends. We were being carried farther from the shore, even Marchand, who was swimming. Then downstream a large canoe, or small sampan, came darting at us, paddled vigorously by four Burmese. I waved, and they came straight towards the canoe. They would be able to tow it inshore with little difficulty, and we could hang on behind.

But on nearing it they changed course slightly, and the rhythm of their powerful strokes did not falter as they drew close, and abreast. I shouted at them. Marchand had ceased swimming and was watching.

One Burmese glanced incuriously at me. The other three preferred to disregard us completely, with no expression on their placid faces. They sped by not six feet distant. They did not stop. In alarm and disbelief I yelled and hollered at their retreating backs.

With sanguine indifference Marchand had commenced swimming again. With a curse I thrust paddles and waterlogged canoe from me and began to swim. But even as we swam the shore receded; and having seen this we continued, knowing we would be lost once we were drawn into the rapid midstream current.

The warring tides dragged us this way and that, sometimes out and sometimes downstream, but always farther from the shore. For long minutes we battled on, fighting against the current with failing limbs.

People had gathered on the shore to witness our struggle. Villagers were assembling en masse, mostly women and children, but there were men among them, and two canoes at their feet. Surely help would come? They would not let us drown, these Buddhists?

Yet as we swam I scanned the shore, and no canoe was manned. Our strength was waning. The river was charged with undertows and malignant currents which dragged at our limbs and sought to draw us under. It was evident that Marchand was flagging fast. His overarm stroke had weakened, and he gasped for air. I drew close to him.

A small whirlpool eddied close to him, drifted beside him and then darted at his head. He was dragged under, and disappeared from sight. Three stokes took me to where he had sunk, and feeling below the surface I found his head and dragged upwards, my hand under his chin. The effort took me under the surface.

With lusty kicking and one flailing arm I propelled both of us to the surface.

He was wide-eyed, he gasped for air, but of fear there was no sign. He was calm, and did not struggle.

"Float!" I rasped urgently. "Relax and float on your back."

Holding up his head with one hand I realised the futility of swimming, and was content to stay above the surface. But still there was no canoe, no help. Marchand relaxed and floated, paddling his outstretched hands, breathing deeply.

Again I scanned the shore and the line of gaping Burmese, who seemed to be drifting upstream. I yelled, waved my arm, I cursed them for the spawn of maggots and pleaded for assistance. I shouted and brayed at the staring throng, and they enjoyed this immensely. It was a splendid spectacle, no doubt, and it was free. It would make a fine story, the two drowning sahibs.

A whirlpool gripped my legs and drew me into its vortex, and I floundered unavailingly as it sucked me down. My movements were slow and tired, it was difficult to swim, and when loose I rose slowly, tiredly, to the surface, and was promptly sucked down again. The river was playing with us. Again I struggled weakly to the surface, limbs aching and head spinning.

Marchand was some yards away, floating calmly still, and inspecting the shore with a cold and stony regard. The vagaries of cross-currents drew us apart. He was taken down towards a headland, and I out closer to the main flow. People were running out to the headland below.

The sky was dark and sullen. A cluster of bulbous hyacinths drifted close, resplendent in delicate lilac bloom. I clutched at it, but it sank, and evaded me.

A fourth time I sank, and again I surfaced, choking for breath and nigh helpless with extreme exhaustion.

Downstream a light canoe was darting out from the headland to Marchand's aid, paddled by a single man. I wondered if someone would come for me in time. I closed my eyes, and tried to breathe with purpose. It seemed an unfitting end, to be drowned before the laughing Burmese. There had been so many other dangers … And no one in the outside world would ever come to hear the truth of what had happened.

Drowned in a stinking gutter of stagnant swamp-flats and festering jungles …

Then I was being dragged under again, slowly, with delicious softness, cushioned by cool waters … My hair was waving like fronds of fern in the water above my head. Then my throat was liquid fire and my lungs were bursting flame, my head was a red mist …

A tight wire bit into my throat and scored my chin, and half-conscious I was pulled to the surface. A man in a canoe had clutched my floating passport-bag as I was surrendering, and I raised my arms to rest them on the stern of the canoe, choking and retching helplessly.

In this fashion he towed me inshore, trailing behind him in the water, waterlogged. In the shallows beneath a multitude of staring faces I lay unconscious with my head upon a rock.

"Are you all right? Hey? Hey?"

It was fifteen minutes later. I was on the bank, lying in the dust but with my head pillowed on some cloth.

"Are you sick?"

It was the doctor. Sick? My head was riven in two at every pulse-beat. My lungs were hot and dry. I wanted to vomit. For minutes I retched and wheezed, then I vomited and fell back dazed.

"You better …see Marchand. May be sick."

"Marchand? Was he with you?"

Why must they ask such foolish questions?

"Yes, yes … other canoe got him. Sick, maybe?"

They all protested simultaneously.

"But no one else was found! Only you."

"What?"

My throbbing head still held the red mist.

"He was with you in the canoe — Marchand? He was not found. Are you sure?"

"But I saw …"

Clearly I had seen the man in the canoe approaching him. He had been saved, of course; perhaps he was on the bank a little farther downstream.

"There was no one else brought in. Only one man was found. Marchand must have gone down in the river."

I gazed blankly at them, and struggled to my feet. Gone down the river? Impossible. Or at least improbable. I had seen the canoe, I told myself. I began walking drunkenly down the river-bank to the headland where I suspected he had been landed, with the assembled villagers herding behind. We went to the headland, and men were asked for news of Marchand.

The man who had sought to save him told the story.

"As I went towards him he just disappeared. He shouted once, then sank, not five yards from me. Something seemed to suddenly pull him under. And he did not come up again. I searched and waited, but he had gone into the main current."

Could Marchand be drowned? Could he be dead? Was he not, then, indestructible? Fatigue bemused my aching brain, and I wrapped my sorrow in the red mist which fogged my consciousness. The kindly Rendier Singh gripped my arm and said, "He is gone, man. It is no use to look."

Marchand was gone. He had drowned.

Four days had passed, the floods had begun to subside.

Dawn was not yet in the sky when I stood upon the headland, under the stars and amid the dew-wet grass. Behind me the westering moon was setting, diffusing its pallid glow on the cotton-wool mists which shrouded the three knolls and hid the monastery from view. The stars were bright, the river before me was profoundly black. One could hear the hiss and gurgle of the turning waters, the restless Chindwin, the seeker of death who sighed for human victims.

Marchand was dead. The debonair, the cynical, the light-hearted, proud and resolute Marchand; the budding philosopher, the youthful sage, the peerless companion. The Chindwin had claimed him, and rendered no return.

I stood alone by the shore, and the moon slid behind the shoulder of a distant hill; Khayyám's moon, falling into India. For a time there was abysmal darkness, and then the early light of dawn climbed in the sky, shedding a cold, pale aura over the jungled hills in the east, over Ye-u, and the road to Mandalay.

Clouds were driving north to darken the light of the dawn. The world was quiet, the sombre clouds hushed the dawn and the lights grew softer, softer, melting to a grey and silver twilight. As I turned to go, the nodding teakwood logs and the covert whispering of the waters mocked me.

Along the road to India I walked, away from the dawn, away from the river and out of the town, alone; and looking down I marvelled that there was so little dust on my shoes.

WHO WANDERS ALONE

PINNEY'S SECOND TRAVEL BOOK, *Who Wanders Alone*, details a dog-legged journey which lasted from September 1952 to late 1953. His longest-distance-between-two-points odyssey meandered from what was then the Free Territory of Trieste (between Italy and Yugoslavia) to the East African island of Zanzibar off Tanganyika (now Tanzania). Much of the time in company of a formidable Dutch woman, Anna, he reached Zanzibar by way of Yugoslavia, Greece, Tunisia, Algeria, the Sahara desert, the Belgian Congo and Kenya.

TRIESTE

Voting day was perilously near when there happened a certain thing which abruptly cancelled my taste for electioneering. We were working with ladders now, cutting Fascist banners down and searching high on the walls for space, since there was none below, and one night when I had put Liberal Party posters over Fascist ones, and was descending to the ground, some villain seized me from behind, lowered me gently to the ground and held me helpless in a powerful grip.

I struggled to be free, but in vain. Who could it be? A Red? A Black? I had seen what they did with the men they caught, and I was filled with fear.

"Ho ho, my brave Britisher! You would put out our little fire?" The Fascist emblem was a tricoloured flame — and this was Mallotti's voice! "You come to play politics? Ho ho ho! You enjoy yourself?"

"Let us not quarrel, *signor*," I said with desperate calm. "I am merely a worker. Let us discuss this thing, like intelligent men. I feel sure —"

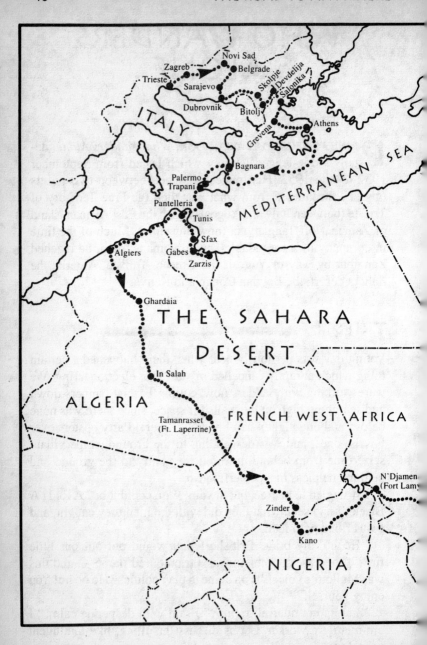

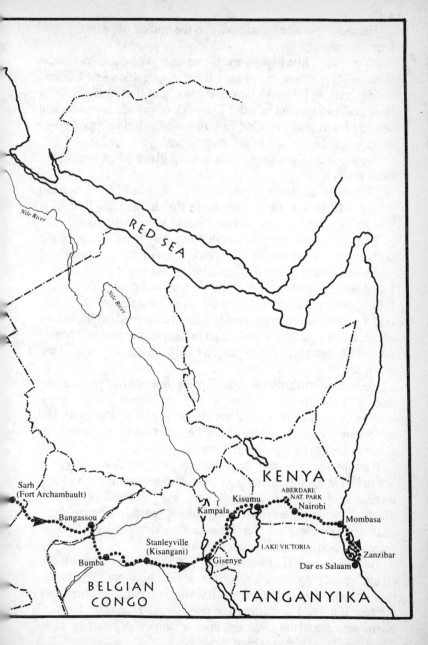

He shook me like a doormat, and the bucket of paste dropped from my hand.

"We do not like Inglesi and Americani who come to meddle with us." He shook me again till my eyes rattled and I feared disintegration. I tried to kick his shins, and flailed my wooden brush behind me, but in vain. The neck of my shirt was twisted so tight I was choking. God help me, what would happen now?

"Do Italians go to London to play with your elections?"

How could I fight such a bull-necked giant, when I could not even reach him?

"It is useless to struggle, *amico*," he mocked. "I am too strong. Maybe you have seen me in the stadium at Milan? Do you know what I will do to you, *amico*? First I will do this …"

The bucket suddenly descended over my head, deluging me with a glut of hot and sticky mess. It swamped my head and poured about my clothes: and the bucket was held down hard as I writhed and twisted. I could not breathe — I gasped for air and fought to raise the bucket. Then the unseen fist slammed fiercely into my ribs and sent me flying blindly: I cannoned off the ladder and crashed against the wall. The bucket clattered away somewhere. I heard Mallotti laughing as I fell, sick and dazed, to the sidewalk.

He moved towards me, but slipped in a pool of paste as he dodged the falling ladder. It missed him by inches, but it was my chance. A cracked rib seared my side with pain as I staggered to my feet and lurched wildly down the street. Mallotti gained his feet and lumbered rapidly after me.

I could scarcely run. My side seemed paralysed. Nausea wrenched at my throat, my legs were without strength. I weaved drunkenly downhill in aimless flight, my head still caked and plastered with paste, my clothes like a melting blancmange. Mallotti was almost upon me when suddenly he grunted in dismay and turned into another street.

Had he gone? Had something …? Then I saw one of the flying-squad jeeps ahead, pulled up at the curb; three American military police were standing by it while their radio hummed and buzzed. But I had no desire to be questioned by anyone, least of all the police, and they watched in astonishment as I hurried past. Then they burst out laughing.

"Holy crap! What in hell was that?"

"A mechanised marshmallow. Straight out of an ice-cream can!"

"Man, these son-of-bitches have more fun ..."

I turned a corner and slunk unhappily away among the shadows, defeated and a fugitive, dishonoured and disgraced, and made my way to the waterfront to bathe, fully clothed, in the sea. I would leave this insane city, I decided.

TUNISIA

SFAX

Abroad in the city after dark I met a Spaniard seeking the señoritas, and went with him to Rue Dar Sabbai, close to the eastern wall. The rest of the city was now deserted, but this street and another were thronged with soldiers, sailors, and town Arabs and bedouins, and an obliging variety of girls — French, Arab, Italian, Jewish, Berber, Maltese, and Spanish, many of them the remnants of a once-thriving white slave traffic, their morals and memories, drowned in tears and dope. Bedouin and Berber girls, strayed from their tribes, or bought, or cast adrift for youthful indiscretions, were decked and draped in finery like high-caste Hindu brides: their ears were weighted with thin gold bangles, and about their powdered necks were silver lockets containing charms, filigree work of intricate design, and heavy necklaces of gold coins; semi-precious stones shone in their raven hair, and extravagant gowns of satin and silk glittered with sequins and delicate embroidery of fine metallic thread: for these tribal women wear their total wealth upon their person, and here an attractive girl may well be rich and almost dead within a year. Others there were with darkened eyes and silver tiaras in their henna'd hair, rings on their fingers and rings on their toes, sultry and smiling groups of them lounging in beautiful clothes on long couches, warming themselves at charcoal braziers and sometimes smoking *kif*, or hashish, in slender silver pipes.

There were shops, too, with oiled and perfumed barbers whose attentions were too suggestive, and stalls where bored youths sold statuettes and postcards surely designed by the Devil himself; one could peer down into lavishly furnished cellar rooms where men in scanty silk attire daintily minced and ogled with girlish mime.

The Spaniard laughed hugely at what he glimpsed in one cellar, and pinched the buttocks of some plump wench who was stroking a soldier's cheek.

"Good streets, eh? Better than those pigs in Tunis. Last night I came here, very drunk. Oh, I was so drunk! In one of these houses I lost the bottom half of my false teeth, but I cannot remember which house I was in. It is bad to have only half a mouth of teeth, no?"

"All the more room for food."

"And twice as long to chew it. I must find my teeth tonight. What shall I say to my wife?"

"What, indeed?" I laughed. He was a light-hearted fellow. He paused to admire a group of four girls, one of whom was playing softly on some stringed instrument. All of them were European, and each of them young and approaching prettiness, as indeed were many in this street; they seemed to lack the barren cynicism common to such people.

"A-a-ah!" A long sigh of appreciation escaped the excited Spaniard. "I like this town. It is a charming place, yes? That leetle blonde there ... I hope I can be able to find my teeth in here."

He would have entered, but at that moment trouble came. Fighting broke out between sailors and legionnaires at one end of the street, and men rushed towards the scene of conflict shouting questions. Courtesans ran to their doors to stare, then began to close their heavy doors and slam home bolts and bars. The noise of conflict grew. The Spaniard suddenly darted inside a coffee-house just before the door swung shut, and while I stood alone, undecided what to do, one of the four girls in the house at my side beckoned, and I went in.

Two of them were French, a third was Lebanese; the fourth was some form of Eurasian, a blonde young woman with violet eyes who made me her personal toy until I revealed the state of my purse; and then she pouted prettily and mocked me for a liar and a priest. The fighting outside spread along the street outside the bolted door, swaying this way and that; the skirmish soon became an Arab versus French affair, with all the ingredients of a first-class "accident", and police came with rifles to force a neutral wedge between the combatants.

The girls brought sweet cakes, and then a hubble-bubble pipe charged with a pleasant mixture of hashish and tobacco; we smoked in turn, passing the long snaking mouthpiece from one to another, and when they had grown a little flushed and bright of eye they danced to music, each again in turn, while one tampered on a drum and a second played a flute. The flute played a softly wailing tune, and the pattering of the drum made me drowsy; but they danced well, and I watched gladly, their skirts a-whirling and bangles clashing — thus they danced each evening when the streets were full, to lure the custom of those who came to watch.

When all was quiet again the door was unbolted and I went outside, and found a place to sleep on the deserted heights of the south-east corner of the town; but I had not slept an hour when one of the *Gens de Maroc* prodded me with a stick and ordered me away. The *Gens de Maroc* are roving night-watchmen who prowl the Arab town in long white robes, an unsavoury form of semi-official Arab police who would rather knock a man to the ground than help him to his feet.

Walking through the streets again I happened on the Spaniard, who was drunk. He had entered some establishment seeking the bottom half of his teeth, but when he came away he found he had lost the top half too, and again could not remember in which house he had been.

Among such coffee-houses as were open I asked for a place to sleep; but when it was discovered I was Australian, no one offered friendship or advice. In New York this day the United Nations had discussed the growing problem of Tunisia, and Australia supported the English, who backed the French. This matter of sleeping being, it seemed, a matter of politics, I announced myself in another street to be an American, declaring I had been robbed by an Australian and stood in need of some kind of bed. Immediately I was offered tea, someone brought me biscuits, and a weaver invited me to sleep on piled blankets in the back of his shop.

Anna had been seen talking to people under the gate called

Porte Delcasse, the main gate of the city, and there I went in the morning to ask for news of her. As I loitered there a shoeshine boy approached and asked if I knew of a woman who wore trousers like a boy; when I replied that I sought this very woman he said he had shined her shoes, and that she had gone to Gabès.

"Did she pay you money to watch for me?" I asked.

"No, but she said you would, if I saw you and gave you the message."

So I gave him a coin and went on a truck south through the desert to Gabès, seventy miles away.

∧∧∧∧∧∧∧

ZARSIS

Anna and I walked south through the desert, chilled by a bitter wind, and rode on various trucks through the bomb-blasted ruins of Mareth and the hives of loaf-like huts comprising Medenine. We rode a tractor into Zarsis, and were walking out of the town to the east, close to the island of Djerba, when one of the Arab mounted police in magnificent robes of gold-edged blue approached and would have delayed us, requiring us to show some form of permit; but we apologised politely and moved on.

Other Arab police pursued us, and since they seemed good fellows and brought us glasses of tea we surrendered our passports and awaited their return from some office in the town. But shortly a French policeman appeared and curtly ordered us to rise and follow him; a meagre fellow, this, with a brisk air of authority and a thin and hostile face. He stared at us with open contempt, sitting on the roadside drinking tea; and when we would have protested he ordered an Arab policeman, who carried a rifle, to fix his bayonet and march behind us. It proved a diverting little procession for the populace, but the crowd who gathered were silent and forbore to jeer.

At the police-station he flipped open our passports. He asked us our nationalities, our ages, where we were born and whence we had come.

"It is all in our passports," said Anna impatiently.

"Enough! When did you enter Tunisie?"

"Oh, ten days ago. Has someone been murdered? Why —?"

"Why are you walking through Zarsis?"

"To go to Djerba. What is —?"

"When did you leave Greece?"

"*Gott verdommen*! I don't know. Months ago."

He sneered. "You do not know? Perhaps you were not in Greece at all?"

Did he think we had forged passports? Were we thought to be *agents provocateurs*?

"You have been to Yugoslavia? … You have both been there?"

A significant point, of course. Doubtless we were Communists.

"And twice to Italy."

That made us Fascists too.

"Why have you been to these places?"

"Please," requested Anna, "do not be a greater fool than you must. We are students who are travelling."

"Travelling on foot, eh? Now, do not lie: how much money do you have?"

The Dutch girl was speechless.

"That is enough," I protested. "It is finished now. We have more to do than listen to the mouthings of a tapeworm like you. We refuse to answer any more of your questions."

We demanded to be set free or be taken to his superior, and following a scene of some bitterness Anna and I were taken to the office of an army captain. Now, the captain was a pleasant and courteous officer who was nervously unhappy to find himself involved in such a dubious conflict.

"The position is this," he explained. "When you were reported to be walking through the village I telephoned to my colonel in Gabès, and he said that as you had no military pass, no right to be here, you must return to Gabès for questioning."

"Colonel Vallah? But we have his permission to come through here!"

The captain shrugged.

"That I do not know about."

The good fellow was persuaded to ring Vallah again, and Anna protested over the phone. But Vallah merely laughed with good humour and said the matter could be discussed at greater length on our return. A mysterious affair. We had come a long way on a hard road from Gabès, and were on the threshold of Djerba. Djerba is the oldest Israelite colony in the world, dating from King David's time, and is said to be the Island of Lotus-eaters and forgetfulness discovered by Ulysses.

"What can I do?" asked the captain. "For myself, I would willingly let you go on to Djerba. A delightful island. But I have my instructions; you must return to Gabès tomorrow. It is too late now. I will call a guide to take you to the Hôtel de France."

"Hôtel de France?" we echoed in dismay.

"But of course. There is no other place."

"Are we under arrest? May we not sleep somewhere else?"

"No, no; you must sleep in the hotel."

"It is your command?"

"I have my orders from the colonel. You are to be kept under supervision."

"Then that's all right. We sleep at the hotel."

There was a four-course meal at the hotel, and a bottle of mellow muscat wine from Kilibia for each of us. Joyously we signed the bill over to Colonel Vallah, and were returned to Gabès in the morning under escort.

The military in Gabès accepted us with suspicious reserve, informed us tersely of the commandant's vast displeasure at being presented with our bill, and handed us over to the civil police for questioning.

Anna was taken to the Commissar of Police, a certain Monsieur Courvarsino, and questioned for two hours while I was detained in a police office under guard in distant Rue Docteur Chavier. After two hours there came the sounds of tumult in the hallway, and I brushed past my guard to witness Anna arriving amidst a tight escort of six police, her hair awry and eyes flashing in a face pale with fury. Her flood of enraged argot was indescribable. She caught sight of me.

"Demand your consul!" she cried. A hand was clapped over her mouth and she bit it vigorously. "They ask a lot of stupid questions and say we're spies and … and …"

"Did you sign anything?" I demanded, and was seized from behind and spun about. She was struggling in the grip of four police as they propelled her towards an open door.

"Nothing. And don't you!" She was thrust roughly into a room and fell on the floor with a thud. Dutch ensued, then a muffled: "Get your consul!"

"Did they search —?" I began, but was thrown bodily into another room. The Chief of Police confronted me in high wrath, demanding to know why I was fighting. Had I been fighting? Well, perhaps I had. My jacket was splashed with blood, and it was not mine. I felt better. Was it the custom of French police, I demanded, to beat up defenceless girls?

Not that Anna was defenceless.

He began asking leading questions, and I asked if I might speak with my consul. He said the phone was out of order. I suggested he was being careless with the truth, and recriminations followed quickly. In my turn I was escorted to Courvarsino's office. The commissar was a round and balding man with thick-lensed spectacles. He had my passport on his desk.

"*Asseyez-vous, monsieur.* Why have you come to Tunisie?"

"I begin to ask myself that. We had intended to go to Djerba to study the life of the Israelite colony."

"With the young girl, eh? She has been most abusive. Where did you meet her?"

"In Athens."

"And you persuaded her to travel with you? H'm. How fortunate … You realise you have no right to be here? That there is a state of emergency here?"

"Then why in the name of the Devil did Vallah give —?"

"You have been in the houses of Arabs. Is that not so?"

To deliver guns or secret messages, presumably.

"Is it forbidden to enter Arab houses?"

"Then you do not deny it. You have eaten food with them. You have been sitting in their coffee-houses. You have travelled with Arab drivers. It is very curious that two Europeans should be doing such things at this time. It has never been done before."

"Then we are pioneers. The first ambassadors of goodwill in a land full of hate and misunderstanding. We shall be honoured with statues in public places."

"And you have refused to pay two hotel bills."

"Two?"

"The young lady arrived before you, did she not? And stayed at a hotel? She did not pay the bill."

"She did not stay at a hotel. She stayed with ..." I stopped myself in time.

"Yes? Where did she stay?"

Very neat. She, of course, had refused to answer this. He would make trouble for her Jewish friends if he found out about them.

"She did not tell you" I asked.

"She refused to answer."

"Perhaps she slept under a date-palm. How would I know? You were here in Gabès, I was not."

"And you have not paid the Zarsis hotel bill."

"Certainly not. We were arrested for no reason and obliged to stay there against our will."

"But you have the manner of thieves! Do you not realise you can be sent to prison for this?"

"Only for a little while."

"And then deported?"

"To a more civilised country, with any luck. *Monsieur le commissar*, this interrogation is absurd. I wish to phone my consul in Tunis before I answer further questions."

"It is quite impossible. The lines are cut and it is impossible to contact Tunis."

Well and good. Consuls have little sympathy for incautious vagabonds.

"When do you expect the lines to be repaired?"

"Tomorrow, perhaps, or the day after."

"Then we must wait until tomorrow, perhaps, or the day after."

They would have to prefer a definite charge, and this would clarify matters.

"You refuse to answer my questions?"

Sneak!

"I wish to speak with my consul."

"You refuse absolutely to answer my questions?"

"I wish to speak with my consul."

He went out of the room for a time, then returned to state: "I have telephoned the *Résidence-Générale* in Tunis, and —

"But you said —"

"— contacted the *Résident-Générale* himself. You —"

"— that the lines were cut."

"— are required to answer my questions. At once."

"Since the lines have been so quickly repaired, you might be good enough to telephone my consul."

"I used the army service. The civilian service is cut and civilians are not permitted to use the army service."

Liar!

"Then, Mr Commissar," I replied in English, "I am afraid I no longer speak French."

A lie for a lie, mistruth for mistruth. He called a clerk.

"You will permit us to search you. What have you in that … that bundle?"

"Nothing of importance to the French government, I assure you. There is a kilogramme of —"

"Show me. And your pockets."

I emptied my pockets and tendered my string bag, for I knew the right was theirs. They dragged out various limp items of food and apparel, examined the few letters and photographs I had, and seized on a notebook with mounting interest. The assistant could read English, and began earnestly translating. The commissar whinnied with delight over certain passages. He became increasingly jubilant. I wondered if they used the guillotine in Tunisia.

They declared the notebook contained subversive notes, and was in fact a report on the political situation in Tunisia.

"You are a journalist," the commissar announced triumphantly. "A journalist spying for … for …"

"For almost anyone. You are free to interpret the situation as your stupidity directs you." I was unbuttoning my shirt. "And even were I a journalist, is there no freedom of the Press in French colonies?"

Abruptly I seized the notebook and thrust it within my shirt. The commissar leapt to his feet shouting. The clerk grappled with me. He ripped my shirt, I ripped his coat. It was most unseemly. The commissar was red with choler, his spectacles fogged with steam.

"Give it! Give it! At once, or you go to prison!"

"To hell!" I cried in anger, but anxiously speculating where all this might lead, and picked up a chair to fend off the clerk. "All right, I *am* a journalist. A special correspondent for the Associated Press of America. And the United Press of Great Britain. And the ... the Amalgamated Press of Australia," not being sure if such organisations even existed. "Be careful, commissar, I have powerful friends in Tunis. The British Consul happens to be my uncle."

What would the Consul have said to this?

The notebook remained within my shirt: and since the commissar could not be certain who or what I was, he suffered me to return to the police office, where Anna and I passed the remainder of the day under arrest.

Arab police intrigued with us. They brought us food and cigarettes, and said:

"You must come back next year. Things will be different then; there will be no French in Tunisie."

They stationed a sentry at the door to watch for French police, and confided in us that they hated the French and only awaited the opportune hour.

"See," they said, showing their empty holsters, "they have taken our pistols from us; they do not trust us, and they are well advised."

"And what of this trouble at Matmata?"

"Oh, there are only forty armed Arabs in the hills out there. Some are men who became impatient and started the fight too soon; others have had their families butchered by the French. Near Gafsa last night the army entered six houses, shot all the occupants, and burnt the houses and bodies with petrol. All because a soldier was shot near by."

"But surely —"

"It is nothing for these people to murder women and children. Everywhere they are killing, killing. They are frightened. Sometimes whole villages are wiped out."

We had no way of telling if what they said was true; but it must be said that Arabs are imaginative historians and prone to embellish humble facts with grandiose lies and legends to their own advantage. The soldiers we had seen had not the manner of assassins.

The Chief of Police appeared once, apparently come to make peace; but Anna would have none of it, though I felt he was not unkind.

"*Liberté, fraternité, egalité,*" she mocked him. "Where does one go to look for these things in Tunisie? Ha! I met the Gestapo in Friesland, in Holland, during the occupation — you see this scar, and this — and I find too little difference in your methods."

Six Arabs, quietly sitting on a bench with dog-chains about their wrists, were interested witnesses of this.

"It is true there are good Frenchmen," one of the Arab police expansively admitted when the chief had gone. "Sometimes their tanks overrun our villages, wiping out whole families in the hope of killing one suspect outlaw. But others I know are kind and gentle, and I have seen soldiers giving bon-bons to Arab children. It is sometimes difficult to know if all Frenchmen should be killed, or only some."

On the stroke of the curfew hour we were locked inside a schoolhouse with no chance to secure a bite to eat: our chattels had been returned to us, and we were told we must leave town, for Tunis, on the early-morning train. We saw eight trucks come through the village bearing many helmetted soldiers, each vehicle with a Bren gun aft mounted as for aircraft, and one truck had a dozen mute and manacled Arabs in it. But for howling dogs, army trucks, and the occasional low laughter of passing Arabs, the night was almost quiet. But one heard the distant crunch of booted feet, saw shadows along the streets: police and soldiers moved in groups, or swiftly in armoured cars.

Too early independence would mean anarchy and disaster for Tunisia: but how long might the lid be clamped on a colony steaming with intrigue and hate?

In the morning an officer came to escort us to the train, but we had discovered the commissar still held some personal papers belonging to Anna; and to his office we went, demanding they be returned.

Argument ensued. The train left. The bus left. At length; the papers were returned.

"Now you must leave at once," snapped the commissar. "You will do well to leave Tunisie altogether." He looked at his watch. "You have exactly one hour to get fifty kilometres north of Gabés. You understand? One hour only. If you are within fifty kilometres after nine-thirty you will be sent to prison."

Anna extended her hands as if for binding.

"The train has left," I pointed out. "The bus has left. Must we run on camels? It will be more convenient to go to prison now."

My notebook was beyond his reach. But he turned his back on us.

"One hour," he repeated. "Only. And fifty kilometres."

We went into the village square to drink coffee at an Arab restaurant, and Arabs, knowing our story, found us a truck to the north. We travelled north past many new road-blocks guarded by police with light machine-guns; curfews had been imposed on Sfax and Sousse.

In Sousse we became separated, and independently made our way by various vehicles round the coast, beyond the Tunisian border, six hundred miles by snow-capped mountains and green valleys to Algiers.

ALGERIA ═══════════════

TAMANRASSET

One night when I returned to my little house I carried no bread, against my custom, for I had gambled with Touaregs for money, and all that I had was lost. They played a confusing game like chequers, but using camel-dung and dates, and though I knew they cheated they moved their hands too swiftly for the eyes of an amateur. I would have to trade my toilet gear, my jacket, and my knife for food … unless a certain plan I had bore fruit.

But disaster walks on two legs: and the second came upon me as I entered my open door, for there stood a cat at bay, its belly

tight with the meat I had saved for my evening meal. There was
nothing else to eat. The cat glared at me and I glowered at the
cat; it hoped to rush past me out of the door. But in a rage I seized
a ten-pound rock and killed the thief stone-dead, then grilled it
for good measure and devoured it — for hunger is a tyrant that
mocks conventional tastes. Cat is cat, and tastes like cat, but I
ate with satisfaction and buried the remains.

How it was I never could tell, but next day the tale was round
the bazaar, and I became known as the Man Who Ate a Cat. How
could they know? I laughed and said it was a lie, but they
declared that two had entered my room, and only one came out.

Since the Touaregs were enthusiastic gamblers, and cheats as
well, I introduced them to an Australian game, played with three
pennies and a piece of wood. One placed the pennies on the kip
and tossed them spinning into the air. I explained that each penny
had two sides, a head and a tail, and when they fell to the ground
there must be two of a kind uppermost, or possibly three. And
men could make money betting on which sides would turn up.
For a time they were suspicious, but when some had been
persuaded to win a few hundred francs (I had borrowed from a
soldier), the others, thinking me a fool ripe to be fleeced again,
swarmed about in a circle with money in their hands. The game
was adapted to the occasion. It was always myself who spun the
pennies. They bet with me for limited sums, and some bet among
themselves; and still I allowed them to win until my money was
almost gone.

Then I raised the limit, betting heads, and hundred-franc notes
were laid on the ground before me in tempting numbers. I had
not the money to cover them, and feared to think what might take
place if my manoeuvre went astray; for a fourth coin now entered
the game, a double-headed penny held out of sight beneath the
kip. When I spun I held one penny with my thumb and let the
double-header fly up in the air with its two honest brothers.

Heads turned up.

I quickly recovered the coins and raked in money. Again I
spun and won, and yet again; then, lest the Touaregs be discour-
ged, I let them win again. But money kept coming in till finally
no man would lay another bet, and with my pocket bulging in a

satisfactory way I went to drink red wine and listen to the
rumours of the Man Who Ate a Cat.

NIGERIA

The native city of Kano, girdled by broken walls and ruled by a
wise Emir, has been a centre of trade for a thousand years and
the goal of great caravans from Timbuktu, Khartoum, and Marrakesh. Lamenting beggars lined the road outside the Women's
Gate as I approached, men in gay pyjamas riding bicycles passed
in and out, and market women walked with silver bangles and
anklets lightly clashing, robed in splendid cloths and balancing
baskets on their heads.

The people all about me were pleasant and polite, and even
anxious to show respect for a man with a pale skin. Some went
so far as to bow to the ground as I passed by. In front of a
butcher's hut was a man with a fire on a mound of ash selling
hot spiced skewers of grilled meat: the meat was studded with
gravel, but here I thought to cook myself some food. Having
purchased half a dozen eggs I queued up at a pump for water,
holding a cooking-can I had brought from Tamanrasset. The
populace evinced surprise, and even consternation, at sight of
one of the dignified *barturi* lining up for water with ordinary
folk. Boys shouted the news of this amusing thing, girls squealed
with delight, and people ran from near and far to crowd about
and watch.

With such dignity as I might muster I filled my can, but
laughter threatened to burst from me when I planted my can, with
the eggs, on the fire in front of the butcher's shop. The crowd
was rapidly swelling, and cries of amazement grew as women
shrilled to the men and the men called their friends. The man
who owned the fire was quite overcome. Someone appeared with
a silver bugle and tootled a series of wild and erratic notes; the
dyers had left their cloth, merchants had quit their shops, beggars
had come from outside the gates, and four policemen paused to
stare in wonder.

A smiling greybeard with a home-made violin pushed close
to play me music, and now the water was bubbling, so I took off

the can and gave the old fellow an egg. The crowd roared with delight. A beggar came to trade his blessings for alms, and since he was a leper — there are many in Kano city — the people made way for him. He knelt to the ground and would have touched my feet, but I pulled him up and he also received an egg, in return for what I supposed to be his blessing. I had no knowledge of these people's language.

Never again would I eat in a restaurant. What king had ever been entertained like this?

But now a smart young man sought to take advantage of the scene. He shouldered his way to my side and with the barest polite preliminaries shamelessly demanded, in the quaint chi-chi English of his kind:

"Sir, I am willing to require three shillings from you. This is because to register myself, and my moneys are not here. The government is requiring three shillings from me, and I am too poor."

I considered him for a moment, a most superior young mountebank in stained white European clothes; stained, aye, and filthy at the sleeves and collar, but in better shape than mine.

"You speak like an educated person," I observed in admiring tones, and he was gratified.

"Sir, I have been to school many times. I am not like these others," indicating the friendly, homely faces pressing close about us. He spoke with an appalling righteousness completely at variance with his request for money.

"You have a house?" I asked.

"Oh yes, I have a house. I do not sleep on the ground."

"A wife?"

"A wife too, Sir —"

"And children?"

"Two children, yes."

"And of course an intelligent educated man like you would not be collecting the filth of the streets."

"Oh, sir, no. I am a clerk. I —"

"Then you are rich," I pointed out, "not poor, as you imagine. I have no wife. No children. No work. And my house is nearly ten thousand miles from here."

"But, sir, every man is knowing that Europeans are rich. I have never seen one who was poor."

Perhaps this was true; he was not entirely to blame. Such Englishmen as came to Kano, came to predetermined jobs, and lived in furnished houses.

"I am not rich," I said, although I had money still. "You see my clothes ..." And I showed him the patches on my shoes. My clothes were tawny with dust. "I am only a traveller, without work. I do not live here."

"There is always work for white men here," he insisted, "with great wages. But I am thinking you are a clever man. You have come, I think, on trading business, and you wear the old clothes of your servant to deceive the merchants into selling to you at cheap prices."

My eggs were growing cold.

"I have no money for you." I turned to go.

Now the young man turned to the crowd and began to make a speech. The assembled citizens listened in uneasy silence to what he said, but one who looked like a fat little friar, in a pale-blue gown with a white rope binding his middle, came to my side and murmured.

"You must go away, at once. He is speaking against you. He says you are a rich man come to mock the poor, and people may believe him."

Here was a thing. I might be torn to pieces by a hostile crowd. To slink away would be dangerous, for flight would admit my guilt. I might be beaten and robbed, if nothing else.

Approaching the orator from behind I stooped down low, seized him by the legs, and turned him upside down so that his legs were in the air and his coat fell about his threshing arms in a rising cloud of dust. His anger knew no bounds, but he was helpless. Silver shillings fell from his pockets, some charms in leather pouches, and a pocket-knife; a silver pocket-watch dangled from a silver chain. I shook him well. A wallet fell to the ground, a comb, a fountain-pen; and people watched astonished to see this mad thing happen.

Then my fat informer laughed, a rich and rolling belly-laugh, and a ripple of uncertain mirth trickled through the crowd. The fat one cried aloud that here was a liar and a fool come to swindle money from a white man, who was neither fool nor liar, when already in his pockets were many important things, including money.

And see how the *barturi* shook him, till treasure fell like autumn apples from a tree!

The crowd was laughing hugely when I dropped the fool among his chattels and went to sit with my eggs and new-found friend under an obu-tree by the Women's Gate. I bought bread from a vendor and we shared the food: to one side the tree three young girls were pounding corn; on the other sat a woman selling nuts.

"It is strange to find a European here," observed my friend, encompassing a peeled egg with a limp bread-flap. "White men stay in the town yonder," indicating the modern settlement a mile beyond the gate. "I have never seen one before who cooked eggs in the market-place. Or," chuckling fatly, "who turned people on their heads. That was a fine thing."

"I have no other place for cooking eggs," I said. "I am a traveller."

"You travel where?"

"East from here, then south."

"To your own city?"

"My city is not in Africa. It is in another place, across a sea, and far from here. No, I am looking for what I shall find in the south, whatever it may be. Men are given legs to move about."

"But people travel for some reason. For business. You are not travelling for business? Then what is your trade?"

"Must every man be saddled with a trade? Must each man be an ant, tutored by convention to kill each day with work? I have no trade. I work when I must and play when I can."

"But all other white men I have met —"

"Other white men have motor-cars. Radios. Homes and wives, clubs and comforts, regular food and fine clothes. They work for money in order to possess these things. I have none of them; But I have freedom, and travel where I will. The world holds too much fascination to waste life sitting in one place."

A troop of black askaris marched past, wearing their boots upon their heads.

"I am a scribe," said the Fat One. "It is work, but I find it is good work which I enjoy. I sit outside the courthouse and write important letters for unimportant people, to the magistrate, or distant relatives, or enemies. I find I am happy doing this, and sometimes when the desire comes to me to sit in another place, I put it from me. Our own weaknesses and false judgment betray us into futile desires and consequent disappointment; but he who finds contentment within himself and is not lured into believing some other state of life to be better than his own, is spared much pain and sorrow."

"You speak as a man who might know a year's contentment, but never a day of happiness. Contentment is commonplace; happiness arises from the unexpected, and in travel one often finds the unexpected."

"A man who is contented should ask nothing more of life," he averred, and wagged his head. "There is a devil on the shoulder of a man who always wanders. Your life must be uncertain."

"Uncertainty breeds doubt, and doubt avoids dogma. Dogma is a tyrant which imprisons the mind with prejudice and obstinate errors. Man was not made to be imprisoned, or even roped to a tree."

He pointed a fat finger at a line of ragged vultures perched like gargoyles on top of the city wall.

"There are birds, free to fly about and visit many places. But are they happy?"

"Who knows?" I pondered. "They are birds."

"Happiness is not a three-legged beast found in foreign places. It is something within one's own heart, to be discovered or overlooked according to a man's perception. It is felt, not seen, like the poverty of the rich."

BELGIAN CONGO

One day I said farewell to friends and went away on a chuffing river-boat which ate its way up-river from one wood-stack to the next, powered each side by threshing paddle-wheels; a grand white castle of a boat brought in sections from the Mississippi. Two men sat for'ard depthing the river with long poles, and ever and anon one heard their melancholy cry: perhaps the ghost of Mark Twain walked the bridge. The steamer felt its way past snags and shallows, weaving through an island maze past villages and overhanging walls of sombre jungle.

A dispute arose about a ticket; in truth I had purchased one, but took the precaution of selling it before I came on board, thinking such a thing might not be needed. At some village I was put ashore and, since meals aboard were so expensive that I could not afford to eat, I was not entirely sorry. A trader in a passing launch took me on up-river, but before the day was done a tempest came and threatened to destroy us. The launch was buffeted by vicious squalls and lashed by stinging gusts of rain. The craft was almost empty. The more we heeled the greater the purchase the wind had on the flat board roof; we were caught on a windward shore, half swamped by rising waves and wallowing drunkenly.

The launch sank gently in the mouth of a creek close to a native village, but the water was shallow here, and the craft bumped and lurched about the sandy bottom with the roof still showing; we had scrambled into overhanging branches as she sank. Natives found us fishing floating objects from the creek and gave us food and shelter; in the morning I walked on through other villages to a palm-oil factory in Elizabetta, and took the road to Stanleyville.

Along this road I overtook a young Topeka girl, wearing some sort of waist-cloth and porting a great bundle on her head. For a mile she walked behind me through the cool morning mists of that narrow jungle road, and then approaching me she asked:

"Lokatu wapi?"

It sounded like "Where are you going?" and I answered that I was bound for Stanleyville. She found this difficult to believe, a white man bent on walking nigh two hundred miles. Her frizzy hair was tightly plaited and she carried a silver charm about her neck, and others about her ankles; the Topeke are a superstitious tribe. To curse an enemy's garden they will throw earth from some grave upon it; at night they only fare abroad in nervous groups and carrying powerful charms, fearing the spirits of the jungle and all kinds of wandering devils. Free love is practised until marriage, but then the moral code is doubly strict.

We paused by a stream, the girl and I, to rest a while and eat my yellow guavas and the sweet palm-tips she carried. A curious conversation was carried on with signs and pictures drawn on the ground, and she made me understand that she wished to be my servant, to care for me by day and bring pleasure to my nights, and live with me in my house at Stanleyville. She refused to believe I had no house, but begged me to employ her and pressed me with various delicacies.

Thumping log drums in every village broadcast the news of the white man's passage, and villagers assembled by the road to await us and greet us, with much laughter and occasional gifts of fruit and eggs, as we passed.

On the following day we were joined by a lad who also decided to go to Stanleyville; he would work in my garden by day, he said, and guard my house at night. So the girl and the boy and I fared on, and within the day an elderly lady with a bundle and a goat had joined my train, enlisting herself to wash my clothes in my house at Stanleyville; and now my staff was almost complete, but I never did manage to find a cook. Two young warriors fell in with the group, so that we were six, but they only came along because they had nothing else to do: and should they decide to go somewhere, the white man could command any truck which came his way. In vain I insisted they should also work: they only laughed and said that they were hunters.

We stayed in a village the second night, where kindly natives, their faces seamed with hideous scars, gave a house to the six of us and brought us eggs. The Topeke never eat eggs, for they think that if they do they will be childless; but I ate ten. The windows were hung with *m'bale* beans to ward off leprosy; one way of catching the disease, it was said, is to be stuck by a *m'bale* bean.

It was a happy house that night. Housemaid produced *qwanga*, a sticky grey mess made from manioc. Houseboy had a parcel of *ponjo*, manioc tubers boiled and meshed with rich red palm-oil. Laundress had fruit and salt and some morsels of monkey-meat, and the warriors carried an ample gourd of toddy. I had purchased a fowl and this was a great success; the Topeke are ever meat-hungry, and will eat any flesh, fresh or rotten, they can find.

A man of this tribe must pay in money or goats for a wife.

When pregnant she returns to her mother's house, and with the birth of each child her husband must buy her back: and woe betide the parents of a child who dies, for inevitably they are accused of killing it, and must drink from the poison cup.

The village was deathly quiet when night had fallen, and even my companions spoke in whispers until brave with toddy-drinking: for it is believed that white men are sorcerers and possessed of powerful ju-jus, and are able after dark to summon the spirits of the dead to do their will.

∧∧∧∧∧∧∧∧

Stanleyville is on the east bank of the Congo, a vigorous and booming settlement bordering the river, with old colonial houses half-concealed among deep avenues and parks. Tropical flowers and fruits are amassed in shady gardens, and neat new bungalows and modern streets attest the bounty of Africa's central jungles.

Except for the girl my retinue had fallen far behind, and now I wondered how I might dispose of her; but when she found I really had no house and could not buy one she slapped my face and stormed the length of a startled street shrilling abuse and inviting numerous curses on my head; and promptly disappeared with a handsome buck in his canoe.

Someone touched my elbow then, and I turned. It was a man who had crossed the river on a ferry with us, a large and well-dressed person in a white sharkskin suit.

"Pardon," he said in French, "could you direct me to the Banque du Congo Belge?"

"Forgive me," I apologised. "I am a stranger too."

"Oh, I see. Are you English? Have you just arrived?"

"On the ferry with you."

"Well. Are you travelling?"

Obviously I was travelling; he must have seen me on the ferry. I marvelled that he did not go; he did not seem the type of man to stop and talk with dusty tramps in the street.

"Have you never been here before?" he persisted.

"Never, *monsieur*. Do I remind you of someone you know?"

"Oh no, no, not at all." Not with patches on my shoes, a dirty string bag of assorted nonsense and trousers torn beyond redemption. "But you see, we Belgians here have a … well, a code of hospitality. Possibly you have no friends here? We like to meet travellers who come to our Congo; would you care to join me in a drink? A little welcome to Stanleyville."

He chuckled ponderously, and I went to sit with him in a splendidly appointed bar. But I did not feel entirely at ease; one learns to mistrust a stranger's drinks. He raised his glass.

"Cheers … A little hotter than London, is it not? How do you find Stanleyville?"

"It seems a prosperous place," I said guardedly. What could be on his mind? The part he played seemed out of character.

"Rich houses for rich people. The natives aren't so well off. Frightful conditions."

He looked at me expectantly. Was this leading to politics? I helped myself to one of his cigarettes.

"Indeed."

"Something should be done about the natives," he continued. "Don't you think so?"

So. His approach began to assume a familiar pattern. I could now be analysed. I was poor, so I must be a defender of the poor. I had not arrived by steamer, or car, or aeroplane, or even by a recognised inner-city route. I had appeared from an unimportant jungle road, walking, a disreputable looking scoundrel with no obvious *cause d'être*. He was thinking I might be a Communist, or some other unsavoury breed.

"I know nothing of the natives," I said.

"It must be interesting to travel about in the jungle. Might I ask your profession?"

What should I say to this? Such an important man would require an intelligent answer. A cleaner of unpleasantness from under cars? No. A yule-tide vendor of Christmas-trees? Certainly not. Such levity would offend him. So I said:

"I am ornithologist. A bird-watcher. I have been travelling in the jungle to study birds." I stubbed my cigarette. I felt sorry for a man who smoked such cigarettes. He watched with interest as I pulled dry native leaf from my pocket and commenced to pack my pipe. He would know I had been in native villages, and of course he had seen the girl.

"Birds," he said gravely. "Yes, there are some strange birds in the Congo. Very strange ones. Did you capture something pretty?"

"I never capture birds. I only observe them."

"Ah. And, er … the girl? She was one of them?"

He eyed me narrowly through a haze of smoke. He was from the Criminal Investigation Department, then. I felt this interview might not last much longer, and finished my drink. He had seen her on the ferry with me, and had followed us. He had heard her shrieking at me in the street, and had put his own interpretation on it. A white man toying with a black woman: an African adventuress abusing a European tramp in fashionable Avenue Reine Elizabeth. An untidy affair, calling for immediate investigation.

"The girl? She found me by a pond measuring the legs of a tufted duck. She thought I was a sorcerer, and was angry because I would not turn her skin white. She was quite mad."

He would take me to the police-station for questioning. The girl had fortunately disappeared, but his evidence could cause me mischief. White man, black woman. The truth would never be believed, for the truth was entirely innocent. I foresaw a month in prison.

I must leave him, at once, before he could be sure I understood his mission. But how could this be done? Was there, perhaps, some other exit than the door? I winced as if with stomach pain, and said:

"Please excuse me for one moment. I fear I have a touch of dysentery."

He rose when I did. "Perhaps it would be better if —"

"One moment. Please." My voice was urgent. He watched me as I went some twenty paces to the rear of the bar and entered the toilet; but after a moment I peeped out, and he was sitting down again, with his back to me but watching the front door. Creeping out I glanced hastily about for some door or window: and cursed myself for a nervous fool, for I had left my string bag, containing several precious things, by my chair. And in any case there was no other exit; no doubt he had known this, and was content to wait.

What could be done? Could I instruct a waiter to call him to the telephone? He was not such a fool. But perhaps … I signalled to a waiter, and requested that he ask my stranger to come to my assistance in the toilet.

"In the toilet, *monsieur*? But if you need help, I may —"

"My passport has almost been destroyed. I need an official witness. Please call my friend, quickly."

I gave him a handsome coin in desperation, and as he walked away, doubtless marvelling at this thing, I padded quietly along behind him and stood behind a palm as he delivered the message. The C.I.D. man asked a question, and after some hesitation went towards the toilet. Snatching up my bag I hurried through the front door and cantered away in the dusk.

TANGANYIKA ▬▬▬▬▬

DAR-ES-SALAAM

Azania Avenue, sweeps from the sheltered township to the sea between pleasant parklands and the sandy harbour margin, a graceful avenue shaded by heavy trees and pencilled with the shadows of leaning cocos-palms.

With unaccustomed dignity I pursued my leisurely way along this elegant drive, dressed with care in a fine grey suit and leading a small black dog on a leather leash; I was freshly bathed and barbered, and my face felt crisp and clean with smarting unguents, a stiff white collar encompassed my throat and a gay bow-tie was fellow to the flower in my lapel.

The day was bright as a day could be, white clouds were sailing high above the interweaving fronds of rustling palms, the water flashed and sparkled between the verdant headlands of the narrow harbour mouth; the town of Dar-es-Salaam lay grey and white and red close behind me, several ships were anchored out and small fishing craft were idling by the farther shore.

Europeans in their cars nodded to me, Africans said "*Yambo*, bwana" "Hullo, sir" — as they passed; I bowed to an elderly lady seated on a bench, and she smiled at me approvingly. Indeed, I was a king this day, and never did a king enjoy it more. Life was a magnificent thing, I reflected, and happiness was captive to the hearts of men, rather than their purses. I paused for a moment to light my pipe, and the little black dog glanced up at me inquiringly. Dar-es-Salaam, the Haven of Peace; indeed, the Arabs who ventured so far from their pirate coasts had named it well, for peace and beauty walked hand in hand in this exquisite anchorage.

Life was absurd and wonderful, each day was without precedent and fraught with strange anomalies; I wondered if I would still be a king at the close of the coming encounter.

On my arrival three days before I had fallen in with a pair of Greeks, and stayed with them in an old and abandoned hotel which they seemed to own. And since I could pass as an Englishman, which they could not, I had gained access to a certain ship in the guise of a shipping agent, and with the steward's aid (he was a Greek) had supervised a deal involving linen, cutlery, and cans of paint. Everyone was richer when the ship sailed away.

With money in my pocket, and wearing borrowed clothes and a borrowed dog, I planned a pretentious approach on the Immigration Office; for I had discovered I could not leave on any boat unless my passport was in order. My temporary Kenya permit was now obsolete; but I was now in Tanganyika, and officials here would have no knowledge, yet, that I had been branded as a prohibited immigrant and commanded to quit British East Africa.

I would ask boldly for an extension of my Kenya permit, valid for Tanganyika; with such a moneyed appearance I could hope to combat or evade awkward questions. I would be a business man, and would portray myself as being about to leave the country, rather than just entering it. Surely they would not ask for a bond? The Immigration Office would now be open, so I turned about and strolled back to the town, and presented myself at an upstairs counter in the Immigration building.

A clerk was attending to a group of anxious Persians; he appeared to be a pleasant and informal person in whose voice I thought I detected some subdued colonial accent. Perhaps he came from New Zealand; he was not Canadian or Australian. Presently he turned to me.

"Good morning to you," I said gravely. "I wonder if you'd be so kind as to extend my permit? I find I have had to stay longer than I expected."

"Yeah ... that's all right," he said. "How long do you want?"

How long? Well, now, I wanted as long as I could have.

"Well ... Suppose I give you a month, then?"

A month? The little dog had made a pool on the floor below the counter. I felt excited too.

"A month would be excellent. Of course I won't need so long, but it will be sufficient to cover all emergencies."

He took away my passport and put another stamp in it. His superior, in another office, automatically endorsed it. I bade him a fond farewell, and marched light-heartedly out of the office.

A month! Here, indeed, was respite. No longer was I hunted, or even a prohibited immigrant; an official extension proved that I was not, I felt sure. I went back to the quiet harbourside, and sat with the dog in a grassy place to smoke my pipe and gaze in appreciation about the fair and shapely cove. For a month I might do as I pleased: but what would be my pleasure? For a year and more than a year I had been moving south, adrift on the open road, seeking the sun and the warm places; and now that I had come so far and found them, might it not be well to rest a while? He who climbs a mountain must rest on top and look about, for there is value to be had in such a pause. Was there not some place where I might idle on a beach, away from men, some pleasant and remote refuge where one could live on fish and tropic fruits and have no care for the morrow?

Coral seas and yellow sands, the trade-winds blowing freely past green shores of drowsy palms; some lonely place, unspoiled by men. ... An island. Aye, an island it would be, of course; and gazing out to sea beyond the palms that laced the harbour mouth, I thought I knew where the place I sought might be:

Zanzibar, the Island of Spice, fifty miles away.

ZANZIBAR

There came a day when I found a beach of such pristine tropic beauty as I had never seen before. It was a long and gentle beach overhung with leaning palms, dazzling white and hot in the noonday sun, fragrant with the smell of cloves and salt and unseen flowers and sibilant with the passing breath of the cool trade-winds. The city of Zanzibar shimmered in the south six miles across blue water, like a horizontal tusk of stained old ivory; the top of the beach was laced with flowering vines and grouped with purple-fruited cactus, the palms were hung with clusters of golden nuts, and mango-trees abounded.

At one end was a whitewashed castle occupied by Indians; at the other end, where a stream ran into the sea, was a grey and weathered *shamba* where a group of Arabs lived. The old coral-stone mansion in the middle seemed deserted, and if it was, then I would live inside it, or build a hut near by — for this splendid and solitary beach was exactly such a place as I had sought. A broken wall of stone hung with creepers and clung with lichen divided the building and its overgrown gardens from the beach. There was no sight nor sound of any human, so I mounted steps from the beach, crossed an open courtyard eroded with age and claimed by grass, and presented myself at the formidable porch. The uprights of a mighty door were carved in orthodox designs, and when I pushed against it one half groaned inquiringly and swung back.

Would there be ghosts? By its colonial conception and advanced state of decay it would be, I thought, a hundred years of age and probably more; and in those days it was the custom to bury slaves in the foundations of any worthwhile house. Carefully I moved about, exploring rooms, not wishing to walk upon a python or a scorpion, or to surprise some hapless ghost.

It was a patriarchal dwelling, solidly constructed and hollow as a gong: there was not a single stick of furniture or so much as an empty box. There were four bathrooms and two of them were Persian, so built that fires could be lit in corners to heat a curious water system; in one of these dim, damp rooms lived a colony of flitter-mice, small bats which squeaked and scolded as I prowled about, and fluttered by my head on softly flapping wings. There was a deep and narrow cell, heavily barred, where slaves used to be kept while awaiting shipment to some other country.

Upstairs a fine veranda overlooked the outer courtyard and the sea; at one end was a room with five great windows, tenanted by swallows and haunted by the wind.

Here, to be sure, was a palace for the most fastidious tramp.

∧∧∧∧∧∧∧

The days were at peace with nature and beyond the touch of humans; there was little to do but idle about the long white beach searching for coloured shells and tracking hermit crabs, or paddle ebb-tide sandbars feeling for mussels with my feet. Beyond the Arab *shamba* to the south was a freshwater stream which merrily gurgled through a forest glade, bordered by tall grass and clumps of fern and watercress. There were oysters on a distant shoal of rocks; sometimes I would cast my fishing-line into the sea and drowse in the sun or fall asleep beneath a palm, with the fishing-line fastened to one toe.

Here, then, was peace; and the misadventures of a maddened world seemed far away.

An Indian came to the house one day and found me sitting by the porch breaking open mango seeds in search of the sweet kernels. This was Mr Tharia, the owner of the estate, a plump and hansome fellow who greeted me uncertainly.

"Hullo yourself," I answered, and offered him some kernels; but he refused them, for he was a Moslem, and this was Ramadhan.

"I heard someone was living here," he said, "in my *shamba*."

"Indeed?"

Village spies, no doubt. If he told me to leave, and locked the house, I would live on the beach. It was a matter of no importance.

"But are you comfortable?" he inquired. "No one has lived here for twenty years. Have you everything?"

My heart warmed to him; he seemed a pleasant fellow. I rose to my feet, munching kernels.

"I have nothing," I admitted, "but I am comfortable."

We walked into the house, which was cleaner than it had been, and I showed him where I lived. My bed was a pile of ferns and grass.

"But you will want a mosquito-net," he assured me, "and a pillow, and a mat to sleep on. A chair. I will bring them for you. Have you enough food?"

I laughed. Such citizens this sultanate possessed!

"This place is ankle-deep with food, and falls down on your head. But tell me, how is it called? What is the name of the village?"

"It is called Bubububu," he said.

I choked on a kernel. "Bu-bu — How many bu's?"

He counted them gravely on his fingers. "Four."

"Bu-bu-bu-bu … But why, in God's name?"

"Well, the Arabs named it thus many years ago. There is a stream near here — you have seen it — which runs into the sea, and the Arabs named the village after the song the water sang. "Bu-bu-bu" … Have you heard the stream?"

"Ye-es, I have …" And of course the Arabs had been right. It was exactly the song the stream sang.

"Are you doing something here?" he inquired. "They say in the village you are doing something here, but no one knows what, or why you do it here."

I chuckled. Sure enough the villagers would be marvelling at what a solitary white man could find to do on the beach of Bubububu.

"I am meditating," I explained, "which is a pleasant way of doing nothing. Perhaps I shall paint a picture, or write a poem, or a book. I am also letting new soles grow on my feet; they have been roughly used too long."

"Well, I will visit you some time," he promised. "I will bring you a mosquito-net, and a mat, and a lamp."

The days grew into weeks, a month; my permit was extended.

A dhow came in one night to the Indian *shamba*, not five hundred yards away, slipping quietly through the night with smuggled goods. Cloth, gold-dust from the Congo, gold bars from South Africa, and Tanganyikan diamonds for rich Indian merchants to salt away in hidden hordes.

Police came again to ask questions. For a time the conversation circled casually about the principle reason for their mission; they laughed pleasantly as they told me of village rumours. It was variously reported in Bubububu that I was a foreign spy, a dope addict, a refugee from justice, a sorcerer.

Of course, the police assured me, none of these things was to be believed. And then came a cunning thrust.

"There is a report," said one, "that you slept in the womens' mosque three nights ago."

I was astonished.

"It is a lie," I declared. "I am not a poon: and their mosque is a century old, and smells. I slept on the beach."

"On the beach?" This interested him. "And, er … did you see something?"

"Something? I saw many things. A mongoose, two bats fighting, a hermit crab changing shells —"

"Yes, yes, but did you see a dhow?"

Ah yes, that was it. They had known all the time I had been on the beach. The secret of the smuggling dhow had somehow been spread about, and someone had seen me that night strolling along the beach: the village had decided I was a smuggler, and no doubt some interesting legend had been noised abroad.

"I saw the dhow," I said. "I think it was smuggling things."

He pulled at his lip.

"We have had information that you are also smuggling, and assisted the crew of the dhow."

"Indeed?" It might have been so; I had little enough to do at night.

"It is a serious matter," he solemnly declared. "There are heavy penalties. Of course, if you deny it, then —"

"I do."

He hesitated, and muttered to his partner in Swahili.

"You see," he continued, "we have agents in each village, and we always know exactly what is happening. Someone must have made a mistake. May we have your word that you will report any smuggling that you see?"

"Certainly not. I am not at war with smugglers. It seems you have spies enough."

He frowned.

"But you will not let them use this *shamba*? It has been used before for such things. Will you give your word?"

"And what am I supposed to do against twenty armed men?" I protested. "Pelt them with mangoes? Surround them? If smugglers come here I shall merely go somewhere else; you have my word for that."

They went away unsatisfied, and I gazed thoughtfully after them.

Late one night I sat on the beach beside the dying embers of a fire, watching a dhow, close-hauled as a dhow can sail, beating in to Zanzibar from Tortoise Island. A fleet of smaller craft called tumbwes were scudding about a shoal of fish two miles at sea; the tide was out, and small creatures were moving furtively about dining on tiny things the sea had left.

A distant ship was passing by to some southern destination; a *m'tepe* was riding the trade-winds north to the coasts of frankincense and myrrh, or beyond. The timbers of *m'tepes* are fastened without nails, being bored with holes and laced together with rope in the manner of a shoe: for the men who sail these craft believe that magnetic mountains on the coast will draw out nails. Constant bailing is required. One can recognise such a craft from the curious bowsprit, curved to represent a camel's neck. The Koran tells of a sacred camel sent from heaven to an ancient tribe of Arabs; but they were a sinful tribe, and killed it, and were punished, so their descendants mould their boats in memory of the beast. A white eye painted on the prow represents the camel's eye, and a flash of red commemorates the slaughter. A white pennant flies from the masthead to represent the power and punishment of Allah, and no other flag may be flown above it.

The melancholy howls of wild dogs came from behind me in the forest, a distant monkey whooped inquiringly. The wind rustled dryly through the palms, and somewhere a flying fox barked harshly in the night.

It was lonely, sitting there. Where was Anna? Perhaps she was working somewhere down in Cape Province — or she may have gone away as stewardess on a ship.

The rice was yellow, the cloves were red. Already the middle of the year approached.

The drifting tramps of southern Europe would be harvesting grapes and revelling in the nights with strong new wine; waifs and strays would be sunning themselves about the Old Port in

Marseilles … In Siam the monsoons would be starting, and adventurous loggers were riding their teak-log rafts down to the klongs and temples of Bangkok; the sparrows in Hyde Park, London, would be drunk and licentious on saffron from clustered crocus-blooms. A seasonal tide of students and vagabonds would be moving up to Scandinavia; the Reindeer Lapps were driving their herds inland from Norway's northern coast, and the wandering Vlachs in Greece would be back in their beloved mountains for early summer.

Throughout the Balkans and south Europe the Rom would be faring forth again in their caravans and cars, slipping over frontiers and sniping fowls from farms — the spoon-makers and bear-drivers, the cardsharps and horse-dealers, the women in their gay green and scarlet dresses advertising occult powers and dancing in the light of fires to stirring ballads lost in ancient lore. The sundowners in Australia were north again for the winter, in Queensland and the Northern Territory, and the post-war crop of restless "seasonals" would be haunting shunting yards, alive with the old excitement to "take 'er on the fly!"

The north-bound dhow was leaning hard before the wind, sails bellying full; I wondered where it might be going. Somaliland, Abyssinia, the Trucial Coast, Baluchistan … It would be interesting, I reflected, to go to the Trucial Coast; something was always happening there. And Abyssinia … A man could probably find his way west to the upper reaches of the Nile. I lit my pipe with a glowing ember, and thought about the Nile.

The last of the dhows would be leaving soon, disappearing to the north like phantoms on the wind of Capricorn.

Soon familiar eagerness crept over me, and my blood quickened. Who could tell what fortune might await a man who travelled on a dhow to Araby?

Besides, the police were becoming far too curious. The day before they had come to search the mansion in my absence, and I discovered them poking about in odd corners searching, no doubt, for bars of gold, or bombs, or a hoard of ivory. They had been unfriendly, when I laughed and joined the search, and all we found were spiders and the nest of a giant rat.

It was time, then, to go. I would leave. I would go away to some distant place, and then beyond, and farther still, until I reached some fascinating land "with pearls as large as pigeons' eggs and ants the size of tigers".

Muscat, Illig, Khartoum, Berbera ...

The moon was low, the night already far advanced; I rose to collect my things and march south under the stars to Zanzibar. A tide of happiness swelled within me. Half a dozen dhows or more might leave today: already I felt the tug of tall, full sails and heard the sea-spray flying across a wooden deck.

Jerusalem, Antioch, Isfahan ... Magic names!

I walked south along the beaches, past the ruins of old palaces, and the first cool light of dawn was pale in the eastern sky as I approached the city and scanned the waterfront. The tide was coming in, the dhows were mincing restively and straining at their ropes.

It is said there is no destination for one who wanders alone.

ANYWHERE BUT HERE

HAVING HOLED-UP ON A BEACH IN ZANZIBAR for three months to write his second book, Pinney hit the track again. During 1954 and 1955 he (again, sometimes with the fearless Anna) meandered back across Africa, from Tanganyika (Tanzania) to Timbuktu. Frequently he had little money; almost never did he have a visa. In the process he transited countries whose names now — only 40 years on — are dim echoes from a colonial museum: Portuguese Mozambique, Rhodesia, Barotseland, Portuguese Angola, the Belgian Congo, Cabinda, French Equatorial Africa, Spanish Guinea, Cameroons, British Nigeria, French Dahomey and British Togoland, Gold Coast, Ivory Coast, Liberia and finally into French West Africa (now Mali) to the middle of the Sahara Desert — and fabled Timbuktu.

TANGANYIKA

"It would have been much better," Chickenthief said firmly, "if we had brought some women with us. Strangers walking in this country without women are looked upon as Government spies, or even police, or worse."

He sighed with honeyed regret, and eased the weight of the bulging sack which squatted on his shoulder. Glancing sunlight rippled on his oily onyx skin as he led the way with leisurely pace across the open plain; scabbed and horny feet scuffed at the narrow trail, so that dust flew forward from his toes and rose in sunshot clouds about his legs. A shiftless worldling from the Seychelle Islands, he had discovered me adrift on some Tanganyikan waterfront spearing mud-crabs with an ancient parasol; and casual encounter had burgeoned into friendship when we robbed a missionary's fish-traps, and fled in delighted terror from the missionary's wife.

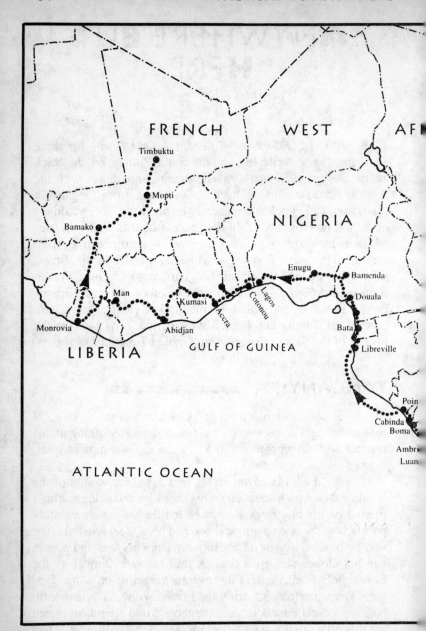

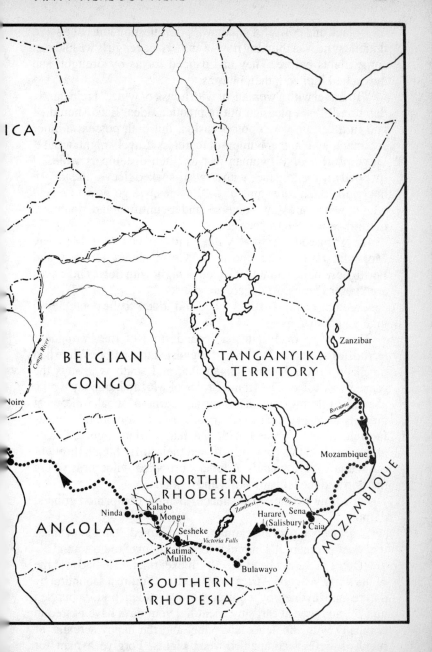

A black and powerful villain with the questing loins of a satyr, doubtless he was thinking now of the two eager girls we had met some nights before. They had danced for us by firelight, and bewitched him with their charms.

"To travel with a woman, or with a cask of wine," I reluctantly demurred, "is a pleasant but impractical idea. Each should be laid in a certain way upon occasion, but both possess a bitter sediment which the bumps of careless travel might arouse. Discomfort sours a woman just as pitch distempers wine." I mopped my melting face with a sweat-soaked sleeve, already we had walked ten miles this day. "Besides, we go now to a land where wines are both diverse and bountiful, and doubtless there'll be women to your taste."

He grimaced wryly. "*N'dio*, and prisons too! Men say Mozambique is a bad, bad place. Criminals are tortured, and Portuguese police hunt black men at night with dogs, and slaves are kept in chains. And there are priests."

"Feeding candles to the wicked and adders to the poor; they'll give you both."

There were many sinister legends told of the Portuguese territories — but the British had suggested that a Poor White had no place in prosperous Tanganyika, and south is always the easiest way to go. The frontier river of Mozambique lay a mile ahead, a glittering drain of swamp and burnt savannah wallowing greasily through the flats to the nearby sea. Low mountain ranges far inland were limned with the harsh white light of early afternoon, and the swamps diffused their torrid breath throughout the hot still lowlands. A lonely, brooding wilderness where the lion and the leopard walk, and demons.

For a time we moved in silence, then my companion grunted damply.

"I am only a poor black man," he mourned, "and I am small without a woman. It's unlucky for a black man to go south."

"Don't make my heart bleed, Chickenthief." He had told me of his thirty years on Africa's east coast. "You're a scoundrel by nature and a thief by choice. You've stolen liquor, burgled houses, and won at cards by cheating; your days have passed in company with indolence and vice, and the happy screams of maidens have accompanied your nights. Forgive a man for asking what prisons you have known, and what kingly sin persuades you to move south to Mozambique."

He was indeed a scoundrel, but a gentleman as well, so he forgave this indiscretion with a happy belly-laugh.

"My sins are small," he chuckled, "so I need not travel far. I merely wish to leave this Mikindani district before the Commissioner should learn I stole a bull, and once across the border I can rest. A man must move away from the smell of his own filth." He purged his nose with a trumpeting snort, wiped his fingers on his shirt, and added enviously, "What crimes you have committed in your native land to cause you constant travel throughout foreign continents I cannot tell, but truly I admire them for what they must have been. Will you work in Mozambique?"

"If necessary, yes; please God it won't be."

"A foolish question," he admitted, and briskly rubbed his nose. "You will commit another crime, of course." His voice rose hopefully. "A great and splendid crime; and I can be your partner. In this way we could buy new wives, and even clothes, and travel to the island of Mauritius. One of my wives is there, or was."

Indeed, we needed clothes even more than we needed wives. Chickenthief was clad in sorry rags, and all his earthly goods were stuffed inside the burlap bag; he wore a long knife at his belt and a red cloth round his head; he had the beetling brow and swollen jaw of primitive Neanderthal man, and looked like a stone-age buccaneer making off with a bag of loot. My feet at least had shoes, though oddly patched and lacking socks; and if my clothes were threadbare too, and dusty, there were sundry small possessions stowed in a handsome paper parcel — and the lady's parasol. The parasol was stubbornly feminine and opened but half-way, yet afforded some protection from this searing southern sun and lent an odour of prestige to poverty.

In a drowsy little village by the river men and women slept in shady places. Only the children were about, fat inklings splashing in the shallows and hunting high adventure in the thickets;

and when they saw us they ran in round-eyed silence to their huts.

"They carry the long, white tooth," said Chickenthief. "See ..."

With lifted brows and a little nod he invited my inspection of the village. The gardens were overgrown with weeds, the fishing-nets were rotten; but there were bicycles, and gramophones, and the women wore new cloth. The Rovuma River was a highway from the elephant country to the coast, and enterprising men with long canoes could carry illicit ivory down to the waiting dhows. Men living in a village whose position held such profit had little need to toil with traps and gardens; and yet it was a sad place. The men had lean, vicious faces, many of them, hungry for something.

One among them rose and slowly came towards us, a tall slope-headed dapperling in vivid cloth, with a spear in his right hand against all courtesy. He drifted to a halt some paces distant; his gaze flickered over us with a lazily critical air, then fixed on a point behind us as if we might have left something on the ground.

"*Yambo*," he drawled, and scratched his bony ribs.

"Salaam," said Chickenthief curtly, not caring for his manner. This spearman was no chief, nor even a village elder, yet one was obliged to accept his bold presumption.

"*Uhn-hun*." The village was a battery of black eyes quietly staring. A naked man lay sprawled in the dust; his back was striped with angry weals, his hands and feet were tied. Chickenthief gazed down the river, then up at the pods of a baobab-tree, and finally fixed on the blade of the young man's spear.

"*Yambo*." He offered a single cigarette, and the spearman took the packet.

"*Ay-ee N'nn*." The tone of his voice suggested weighty thought and wise decisions. He avoided my eyes and stared at the parasol. "*Yambo*?"

"*N'dio*." Was the man in the dust alive, or dead? Ants were at his wounds and flies were in his mouth; he must be dead. "*Yambo*. Salaam. H'm." I jingled a few shillings in my pocket and glanced across the river, wondering what to pay for a canoe; if they suspected we were fugitives the price would be too high.

The stranger nodded agreeably and shifted the spear to his left hand.

"*N'dio. N'un.* Salaam."

We were accepted, then, as travellers who wished to cross the river; and since visitors embarrass those who harbour guilt, we were granted a canoe, without cost, and were poled across the river to the shores of Mozambique.

MOZAMBIQUE

The crewmen set us on a grassy bank pressed to the river margin by a formidable phalanx of elephant-grass; up-river were islands brightly daubed with colonies of birds, and far downstream three crocodiles slept on a sandy bar. The canoe turned back; Chickenthief shouldered his burlap bag and grinned expansively.

"Now my sins all lie behind me," he observed.

"Your sins lie in your heart like sleeping maggots. God help you when they wake. Lead on."

Chuckling to himself he turned to the muddy trail which tunnelled through the grass, and soon we were engulfed in a sibilant, scraping shadow-world of hot and prickling gloom. The constant passing of men and beasts had gouged the trail to a channel of black slime, and as we waded knee-deep in morass the odours of rank rottenness reached up with oven heat, and perspiration pulsed forth on our saturated hides. Would there be crocodiles? Devils in the slime were plucking at my shoes. Doubtless there were leeches, ticks, and grave-worms, and other foulsome things.

Why was I here? What manner of fool was a man who abandoned paradise on the glamorous Spice Islands to stumble along a festering drain on the ulcerous edge of the world?

A dozen trails led out of the swamp in as many different directions, patterned with the giant spoor of elephant and hippo, and the lesser wading birds and deer. We found ourselves in ancient gardens; beyond were baobab-trees scattered about a rolling plain.

"Each man to his trail," said Chickenthief, scanning the broken walls of tall savannah. "We travel between the sea and the hills, south across the plain. There may be lions; let us keep close to the sea."

Ten miles south, beyond low hills matted with dry scrub, we came upon the father of all swamps. The tide was now in flood, and cut by deep black channels snaking among the mangroves; and even as we waded through, or swung across on branches, my stomach chilled at sight of crocodiles. The shadows of dusk closed in as we waded through the gurgling tide and avenues of mud; another hour and nightfall would maroon us. A devilish place; the haunt of savage creatures come, perhaps, for salt, and the lair of many crocodiles which hunted the tides for fish.

"Chickenthief!"

"Oh?"

"Let's get to hell out of here."

"The trail bears west. Are you afraid?"

He walked with a demon on his shoulders, this villainous Bourbon Creole, and fear was a jest to plague a tender maiden. If the trail bore west it would leave the swamp.

Soon the swamp was behind us, and for a time we walked in twilight west and south; we might reach the frontier outpost of Quionga in the dark. Something came rushing through the shadows and passed us in full flight. A wild pig. Two startled deer skipped by and dashed into the swamp.

"Ho," called Chickenthief, "perhaps we should climb trees. Some animal is hunting, and if we walk it may hunt us."

"I am already in a tree," I said, gazing down reproachfully. Only fools and warriors walk about with lions and leopards. He was laughing to himself as he climbed to a lofty perch, and I grinned delightedly when ants pursued him through the branches. No beast came; except for the sound of Chickenthief crunching manioc the night was almost still; I nibbled on a kola-nut and smoked a little hemp, and firmly wedged myself in a treble fork.

The night was catalogued with fitful dreams. We would reach Quionga in the morning, and a road would bear us south to somewhere else.

∧∧∧∧∧∧

Somewhere beyond Sena, up the river, I swung aboard a freight at night, alone and unobserved. The night was cool and growing cooler, and there was far to go, so finding a pile of empty bags in an all but empty truck I burrowed in and sat with only my head exposed. For fifty leagues up-river there was no road at all, so a man might be forgiven for borrowing a train; and there was at least one other who planned to ride this freight. He climbed cautiously aboard at the second siding, an African wearing a shapeless hat and a ragged army coat.

He dropped quietly on all fours to the floor of the truck, and by the light of a distant yard-lamp one could see him crouching there, tense as a nervous deer, reading the sounds of the night and alert for trouble. He would be severely punished if they caught him. As the train commenced to move he scuttled towards the mound of bags; but several feet away he paused, and the whites of his eyes were showing as he sought to identify the sinister object on top of the heap.

A passing yard-lamp filled the truck with harsh illumination … and suddenly he saw a white man's bearded head impassively regarding him from a distance of three feet. His eyes bulged, his mouth fell slack. With an anguished howl of superstitious terror he bounded out of the wagon and was swallowed by the night.

Walking towards the border on an empty sunset road I marvelled that shabby cities could beguile the hearts of men. The woodland was at peace, and small creatures were about, flitting among the cloistered columns of tall trees; squirrels darted in mock panic about the forest floor, birds were singing vespers in the branches. The odour of herbs and dying blooms haunted the mountain air, the sun was low and the shadows of dusk lay deep and cool across the road; it was a pleasant thing to walk amid such scented solitude, and the sack across my shoulder accompanied my movements with the gentle clink of bottles, a sound more pleasing than the song of any bird. Wine, some wise man said, hath its own music, sometimes referred to as the music of tall spheres; from my shirt I took a bottle almost emptied by the rigours of the last few miles.

The furnishings of the freight train had reflected high credit on the friendly Portuguese: for in one of the trucks, invitingly displayed and unattended, there was such a store of crated wine as might have gladdened the heart of any king. Assuming possession of an empty bag I had stowed six bottles in it, and set out well provisioned for the long road to Rhodesia.

A deep, sweet draught evoked a sigh of satisfaction. Wine, red wine … it was good to be on the open road with such fine company.

But what was this? A thread of faraway music was weaving thinly through the twilit forest, elusive with distance, rising and falling like a breeze softly fluting on the pagan reeds of Pan. It seemed to pause, and then commenced again, a wanton woodland barcarole of silvery caprice. Was this some enchanted glade? Did leprechauns and dwergers inhabit the Mazoe Hills? Perhaps some comely sprite would come to share my wine; or were they demons? A toast was drunk to demons; and, with the cunning of the wine running richly through my veins, the parasol held ready as a sword, I crouched and stealthily stalked the source of music. It seemed to come from behind a great baobab-tree; hard against the bole I paused, and carefully peering round the other side beheld as curious a scene as one might happen on in any enchanted place.

By a smouldering fire a dreamy coon sat singing softly to a crude mandolin, his eyes closed in rapture. At his side was a second man who sat with out-thrust legs; between his two big toes were stretched three cords, and on each cord was a little black doll which danced when he wiggled his toes. They danced to the mandolin, jiggling to and fro and up and down, nodding and bobbing as the two big toes wiggled to the music.

Well, here were two jolly fools! They would entertain me, I would give them wine; with my liquor and their clowning we could pass a pleasant evening in these pixilated woods. One must be careful lest one's too abrupt appearance should frighten them away; but even as I withdrew my head, the man with the three dolls saw it.

There came the sound of excited shouts and a sudden flurry of movement, and peering round the tree again I perceived the doll-man trying to flee with his toes still tied with string. He fell, and rose, and fell again, shouting in fear and protest, while his friend stood gazing after him in wide-eyed disbelief. There was nothing one could do but step from behind the tree with an inoffensive air, and casually greeting the second man I squatted by the fire. He was made of sterner stuff this one: after fidgeting uncertainly for some seconds he sat down again, and finding this new and harmless Beard could not speak his language he turned once more to his mandolin.

The doll-man, who had been sitting on the ground at some distance untethering his toes and watching us, now returned, but stood nervously rolling his eyes and muttering to his friend until a bottle of wine had passed round; each draught was greeted with friendly grins and an accolade of belching.

Scarcely had we finished the first bottle when the doll-man turned and stared into the night: someone, deep in the woods, was tampering with a drum. A second drum broke in, and then a third, until the forest was loud with waves of muted thunder, and with scarcely a word we arose and set off towards the drums and the rising moon.

In a small village of round grass huts men were dancing on a miniature arena of packed earth, shadowy figures shuffling and bounding in the light of two log fires. A battery of six drummers squatted by one fire with other men, the women sat round another fire singing and clapping their hands in a slow and steady beat which somehow harmonised with the rapid, broken rhythm of the drums. A place was made for us; the drummers grinned their greeting, an old man passed us gourds of cashew cider, others nodded and leant forward to shake our hands. Men whispered delightedly among themselves when a bottle was brought forth from my bag; it was clear they appreciated white man's magic.

The first dance ended, the drums fell quiet; I settled comfortably on a log and politely puffed my neighbour's pipe; that cashew cider had an unpolished potency, and only those who proved unworthy of the brew would sleep tonight.

The master drum performed a *tour de force*, and a warrior leapt into the empty ring with thudding feet and stabbing spear: his face was painted yellow and red, and he wore a waving head-dress woven of coloured grass and beads and shells. Five other drums came in, each with its own contrasting rhythmic pattern cunningly interwoven with the master; other warriors entered the ring and began slowly dancing in a circle, heavily stamping with two pulses to each foot and holding spears aloft, oily hides glinting and rough with the lumpy weals of tribal scars. A musician with a xylophone riffled up and down his scale, opening up the magic it possessed, and other xylophones came into play, small hand-pianos, treble and bass and double-bass and highly resonant: and now the girls slipped through the men and formed an inner circle, protected from the enemy and exhorting their men to war. Slowly they danced, with whispering feet, their bodies rippling top to toe, skirts a-quiver and bosoms trembling, richly polished by the firelight; then faster, faster yet, hammering the ground with frenzied feet, responding to the hypnotising tempo of the drums.

There was a dance in which two men were dressed as roosters, heads and shoulders and loins tufted with black feathers, and they courted a squatting woman who played the part of a fowl. Hunched low on their hams before her and moving to the softly thudding drums they stimulated the arrogant strut of cocks, sometimes darting at each other with feathered arms like angrily downstretched wings. The woman clucked and swayed and timidly turned her tail from the amorous approach of either cock; but one of the rivals fled before a vicious onslaught of beak and spur, the victor danced before her with plumes excitedly shivering to the rapidly increasing tempo of the drums, and the natural conclusion of the dance was greeted by delighted screams from the women, shouts of encouragement from the men, and such a volley from the drums as shook the ground.

The night wore on. Each man insisted I share his drink and gratefully shared the wine, and by the time the bag was empty, and the moon low in the western sky, the fires were moving uncertainly and the faces all round swayed and doubled and disappeared in a most confusing manner.

The doll-man and his partner lurched dizzily into the ring, capering on undisciplined legs; and using the parasol for support I joined them in an odd and complicated dance which ended amid a burst of tolerant applause and a ringing tribute from the drums; and he who was presumably the chief, and who sat on a hippo skull, came forward to present me with a chicken.

The sun was high and the drums were throbbing still when I

Pinney framed in a window of the great citadel in Aleppo, Syria, late 1948

With his early travelling companion, Robert Marchand, Pinney crossed Syria and Iraq in early 1949. As ever, they countered (and provoked) local bureaucratic obstructions with a good deal of ingenuity and impertinence.

The Naga villages of Assam's Smora Tract, close by the Burmese border, were fortified by palisades of sharpened bamboo stakes. Pinney and Marchand trekked through here in mid-1950, illegally exiting India and entering Burmese head-hunter territory.

"We had to go without visas. We ran away from arrest at Kohima in Assam, and snuck out of Pek before dawn to elude the garrison. Then onward east through jungled mountains, via Naga villages: laughing virile, happy folk who were generous and helpful to us."

Bob Marchand makes his way carefully across a cane suspension bridge above the Ti-ho river in Assam, north-eastern India. From this point, he and Pinney left behind the relative safety of the administered territory for the fearsome jungle terrain and customs of tribal territory.

"We marched deeper into the mountains, knowing nothing about the land ahead except that we'd bump into Burma if we kept on far enough. One morning we came to the edge of the Somra Tract and crossed the Ti-ho River gorge on a swaying kunda bridge: this was the limit of the law. On the other side was Unadministered Territory — where government patrols did not venture, a mountainous wilderness where the tribes were accomplished head-hunters, and feared as raiders and assassins. And Marchand was completely fearless."

After Marchand's death, Pinney was deported from Burma to India.

"The Burmese officially listed me as Criminal No. 13 of the Upper Chindwin District, and demanded to know at what point I had entered Burma. Point? They could not savvy that I had crossed over a mountain, entering at a point lost in rain-forests and perpetual mist. They insisted there must have been a village or town … and so I invented a Burmese Bullamakanka for them, and described it, and told them how many people lived there (99 except once a year when Santa Claus came). I pointed out its exact location on a map, and they marked it in. Perhaps on future maps Bullamakanka would appear as a Burmese border post, and would be asked to pay taxes."

September 1952 found Pinney back in Europe, entangled in the election campaign of the Trieste Free Territory. His career as a poster paster came literally to a sticky end when he was attacked by a giant Fascist.

Wherever he was, Peter Pinney often ended up in the local bazaar, buying or selling whatever he could, sometimes even trading his own clothes for supplies.

Trieste. The starting point of Pinney's next epic journey, which led to Yugoslavia and Greece, crossed the Mediterranean and then traversed Africa from Tunisia to Zanzibar.

Passport inspection, Yugoslavia, 1952. For Peter Pinney "bickering with the Law was a natural corollary of travelling", and he had plenty of practice at it.

"Yugoslavia proved to be one of the most beautiful, diverse and fascinating countries of all Europe, and one of the friendliest — but the police were a pain in the arse. They were persistently suspicious of a hitch-hiking stranger, a foreigner on foot, a 'studentski Avstralensk' who squeezed all his luggage inside a string bag."

In 1954, Pinney and his travelling companion, Anna, crossed Africa from east to west. "Anna was a Dutch girl, dynamic and petite, like a leopard. Association with her was spiked with small adventures, and she had a temper like a split fuse." In Kalabo, in the kingdom of Barotseland (now the Western Province of Zambia), they fell in with a troop of local musicians.

With Anna on the Cuanza River, Portuguese Angola. For three days Pinney and Anna paddled downriver to Luanda on the coast.

In Angola, late 1954. "Wearing a Scottish kilt presented by Covent Garden Opera Company staff (in Rhodesia), and toting a rug of animal skins, the Africans thought I was some sort of bearded lady, and Anna confused them by wearing trousers."

In French Equatorial Africa (Gabon). "We struggled for two weeks through swampy coastal lowlands north of Libreville, we were obliged to claim we were smugglers to win the trust of strangers, and were deported from Spanish Guinea to countries for which, likewise, we had no visas."

1962. On board the passenger ship *Tahitien*, between Tahiti and the New Hebrides (Vanuatu). In the foreground is Cliff. From the left: Lance, Pinney and Denny.

said farewell and, bearing the chicken in my bag, turned back on to the road towards the west.

BELGIAN CONGO ━━━━

Great things there are on earth. Glaciers poised in the womb of Time, volcanoes born at sea, the Painted Desert, the Midnight Sun, the Navel of the Ocean off Hittezen, and avalanches creaming in white thunder from Himalayan peaks — but few are more impressive than the marriage of the Congo with the sea. The river rises from a thousand cataracts and swamps, from the valleys of Mitumba and the Mountains of the Moon, swelling to a powerful giant embracing countless islands, draining a million square miles in the jungled heart of Africa, and surges south and west, south and west, looping, twisting, wrenching jungled islands loose and spewing them over rapids, then forges strongly through the lowlands and thrusts into the Atlantic in a purling spate of cloudy amber more than five miles wide.

The Mother of the Sea, Augusta had called it.

Anna and I had crossed the river by canoe and landed secretly near Boma, forty miles up-river, and ridden with a Belgian in his Chrysler to the coast, and now we stood in a high place with the jungle at our backs and gazed down on the river and the sea. The river held tall islands daubed with European settlements, curiously akin to medieval strongholds set as for defence on moated hills; the sea was stained with a great brown stain which spread to the horizon.

"It is a place," said Anna.

"It is a place, indeed." From association with her one realised what she meant: that this was one of the prizes which made the road worth while.

"I am happy we did not try to cross down there," she murmured. "That water would eat a small canoe … this is the second time I've seen the Congo River, and I think the last."

She saluted the river with a kiss, and we turned to follow the road north to Cabinda.

Night was falling as we drew close to the border, and we would have walked round the Belgian frontier control under cover of the darkness, but an *askari* on a bicycle had overtaken us and insisted on leading the way. He was puzzled to see white people walking with their luggage on their heads, as we had learnt to do; and indeed this unconventional manoeuvre had caused dismay and laughter among many of the whites who saw us pass, but days and nights of bearing burdens in our hands had caused our shoulders to be hostile to the weight, so we followed the native custom and it served us very well.

The frontier post consisted of several native huts and a small brick building with an office; beyond were two white posts with a chain between them across the road, and on the other side lay Portuguese Cabinda, and a handsome house. We had entered the Belgian Congo and crossed it, merely a narrow corridor which gave the inland access to the sea, and all that remained was another hundred yards. There were no white officials in this Belgian frontier post, only native clerks, policemen, and *askaris*; and the arrival of two Europeans on foot, a girl in pants and a man in a skirt walking through the night balancing bundles on their heads, and bearing all the signs of distant travel, was almost too much for the passport officer. He stood in the doorway of his office gazing in astonishment, then advanced with hand out-stretched for passports. Two clerks and a policeman came behind him.

"You go to Cabinda? On foot? Please, I must see your passports."

But when it was discovered we had only one between us, and that without a visa or even an "entry" stamp, there commenced some formidable horseplay which waxed vigorous as other officials and *askaris* came with important-looking documents and old-fashioned rifles, swarming about us like ectoplasm at a witches' sabbath and whinnying with light hysteria. They corralled us in the office and fired excited questions at us and at each other, while clerks and cooks and corporals pressed close to the door discussing the significance of two Europeans walking in the night, with their baggage on their heads and no proper papers, to this most important border.

"You have one passport only? And no visas?"

"We have three passports and a hundred visas. See." My three passports were bound together; two were full of stamps and visas, and third was now in use. "Of course the lady is my wife."

The lady winced, and whispered something rude. Half a dozen different men thumbed slowly through the passports, staring in vague wonder at successive pages crowded with the licences and legends of governments and consuls. They found an old visa for the Congo, ten months stale, and closely studied it.

"You see, we have a visa. Our passports are in order."

They were candidly suspicious.

"But how long have you been in this country?"

"Only a single day. We have come from Angola."

"One day? And all the way on foot?"

"A policeman brought us half-way in his car."

"And where is the entry stamp? There is none."

"It must be there somewhere. Sometimes they move about; and it is difficult to find one among so many."

They were not satisfied. Something was amiss. The lady had no passport, the man's visa was quite old and already used; they had been discovered sneaking towards the frontier at night like fugitives; and on foot. There was the thing: Europeans never walked on foot like common coolies.

Doubtless they were spies. *Espion.* The word was tossed to and fro in whispered asides. Communists! *Agents provocateur!* The chief clerk locked my passport in a drawer, and pocketed the key.

"We must telephone Banana," he announced with fine authority. "You must stay here tonight, and we will telephone Banana in the morning."

"I think we must find horses quickly," Anna murmured, edging towards the door. "Get your little book."

Our baggage was outside. Something would have to happen soon, at once.

"Let me show you something in the passport which you did not see," I suggested wildly. "In Boma the police wrote something in it, a special thing which you did not see."

Anna was moving casually through the crowd which blocked the doorway, commanding them to move aside, and this they did. Reluctantly the clerk unlocked the drawer, pulled out the passport, and handed it to me. I thumbed through several pages, consumed with anticipation of the thing which must be done, and filled my lungs with air.

Suddenly I shouted and flung my arms about me madly.

"Warrrgh!"

Officials scattered and bodies fell as an obvious maniac hurtled across the office and cannoned through the door. Someone seized and ripped his shirt, but he was already gone, snatching a bundle from the ground and plunging through the darkness after the rapidly scudding girl. An armed *askari* from the road sought to intercept us, but Anna swung her valise at his head and I pushed him off his balance in swift transit. Bedlam had broken loose behind us: policemen, clerks and *askaris* gave tongue and came pounding through the darkness. We hurdled the chain across the road and galloped across the border to Cabinda.

The Portuguese house was close to the road. Senhor Sores and his wife were having dinner, and were taken completely unawares when two panting strangers dashed up their back steps and into the kitchen, slamming the door behind them.

"*Pardon, monsieur, madame!*" Anna puffed an apology. "*Pardon mille fois.*"

"We have visas," I added quickly.

"We are hunted by Africans. Excuse us!"

The *senhora* gaped, her spoon poised in mid-air. Senhor Sores rose, wiping his mouth, and grasped a shotgun near at hand.

"What happens?" he asked in French. "What arrives?"

There were shouts outside, and someone hammered on the door. Briefly the position was explained, or as much as would seem prudent.

He strode to the door and flung it wide. A score of natives were gathered outside demanding their pound of flesh.

"*Allez!*" he shouted. "Go! Get back on your own side of the border or I'll have you all deported! *Vite! Allez!*"

With a shotgun in his hand he dominated even the *askaris*. They moved away, muttering among themselves and flinging threats and taunts across their shoulders.

"Bandits! *Blageurs!*" growled our new ally, and slammed the door. "Please, be seated. Have you taken food?" He waved aside the passport and poured us wine. "They come at night to steal my guinea-fowls," he said testily. "They steal my chicken-wire.

They are monkeys with rifles and rubber stamps, pretending to be civilised, and always making trouble."

We dined with them, and they gave us mattresses and blankets for the night.

"In the morning I will take you to the township of Cabinda," he promised, "for I must, of course, see mademoiselle's passport, which you say is waiting there, and put my stamp in it. Then everyone is happy, and there is no more trouble."

FRENCH EQUATORIAL AFRICA

The way led through rich deep jungle shrill with the insistent canticles of crickets and the cries of unseen birds, and brought us to a rapid steam bridged by a giant log. A man was squatting on the log doing some strange things. His face and body were painted in loops and whorls of red and white, and he was quite naked except for strings of improbable objects hanging from his neck, and odd-looking fetishes tied to his arms. He was chanting softly to himself and carefully laying blades of grass across the top of the log; and he had a string about one ear, with a nut suspended from it, and when he wiggled his ear the nut bobbed up and down.

"He is mad," I whispered. We had paused some yards away and stood observing him. "He was left behind when everyone went away, and now he has gone mad."

"No, he is making magic," she murmured. "He is putting voodoo on the bridge."

He had turned his face upstream, and addressed the water in a crooning monotone. In the shadows beyond the bridge we could see a group of spearmen, but we were shielded from their view. Were these the men who had broken the peace of the night? Did they think that we were ghosts, and were they seeking to bewitch the log so that we could not cross? What would happen when they saw us?

The man on the log tore a necklace of coloured shells from his throat and threw them in the river, and turned again towards us to lay more blades of grass. We cautiously advanced, moving slowly, wondering how we might establish friendship: and suddenly he saw us.

His eyes popped and his mouth fell slack.

"*Arrrrrh!*"

With an agile bound he leapt into the air and turned to seek escape, but slipped and fell spreadeagled on the log. The warriors were instantly in flight. He scrabbled wildly at the log, then found his grip and scudded over it, flashed into the jungle and was gone.

"He thinks we are funny things," she said. "What must we do?"

"Let's cross this log before it vanishes, or turns into a bird."

"It is not pleasant to walk on logs so recently enchanted, but we passed across without unnatural trouble. Far ahead along the trail we could hear thin cries and shouts, and the whinnying of women; and in less than several hundred yards we came upon a village. It had been rapidly abandoned. Pots were bubbling on fires, fowls were clucking nervously in sequel to high panic, mortars and stools were overturned, and a lazy film of dust was slowly settling in the single village street. No man, woman, or child was to be seen. The trail abruptly ended on the bank of a tidal river, and on the other side were mangrove swamps. Anna was moving from hut to hut and peering into pots, exclaiming with critical delight at what she found; but I was nervous.

A volley of spears, a hail of gunshot … we were not welcome, we were enemies, and feared.

"Pietr, there is rice, there is fish, there is *bouillon*, mock-turtle soup and nice potatoes."

A head ducked out of sight behind a tree. A twig snapped near at hand. A bush began to tremble, and someone with enormous eyes peered from behind it. God spare us, we were surrounded: would they attack? Anna was busily spooning something from a pot, and making small noises of contentment; for a while I dithered, then went to join her; it is said one must never die on an empty stomach. We sat in the doorway of a hut feasting on rice and fish and white meat, spitting the bones and dross in the dust in approved Temboni fashion, and then found a calabash of beer.

It was a crude and muddy swamp beer, made from the juice

of palms and sugar-cane, rich and sweet and full of pounded fibre, with a highly individual bouquet; and it served the moment well. Confidence returned. We found a couple of drums and began to beat upon them, and filled the air with the chilling cries of Indians a-scalping, pounding out a challenge to the jungle, to warriors and demons and whoever might be there: and soon enough the warriors appeared. They were reluctant to believe that fully accredited spirits would invade their homes and eat their food, and drink their beer and sing, and hammer bouncy rhythms on their drums; for spirits are not supposed to do these things. And now they advanced in a body from the forest, clutching spears and axes and approaching circumspectly, muttering and whispering and urging one another on with bold assurances.

We pretended to ignore them until they were quite close, then turned and greeted them with smiles and friendly signs. Several among them had some words of French. Confidence grew and flowered on both sides; then Anna, being Anna, took an egg out of her pocket, made magic passes over it, and rolled it along the ground towards their feet.

Half the assembled warriors fled. Others, more adventurous, stood their ground and gripped their spears, and hissed fiercely at the egg. A magic thing! They stared at it, and stared at Anna, who was grinning impishly and trying not to laugh. One of them nudged it with the point of a long spear, and turned it over, while the others watched with alarm and curiosity.

Then Anna and I began to laugh, and we could not stop. The spearmen watched in silence, then slowly their frowns relaxed and they began to grin; and someone giggled. Soon the whole crowd was convulsed with delighted laughter, and when they all began to dance about the egg, brandishing their spears in mock attack and doubling up with laughter at their own timidity, we seized the drums and gave them some hot rhythm.

Someone finally jumped on the egg and killed it.

The chief was one among them, a grizzled little gentleman broad of brow and bow-legged, with the weals of heavy tattoos on his face and arms and chest. He greeted us with courtesy, when the egg had been properly killed, and took us to his house to dine again.

He pressed us to stay in his village for the day, and so we did, and drank swamp-beer till the moon was high and hazed with creeping mists. In the morning we were taken down to the coast in a canoe, through dim and rapid channels overshadowed by tall trees and hung with clutching vines, a shadowy half-world of sudden corridors and tunnels throbbing with ghostly echoes and pierced by the startled cries of scavenging birds. Large dark birds flapped softly past our heads, fish splashed and plopped beside us; natives in canoes paddled in and out of quiet byways, setting snares and bearing prominent fetishes to ward off evil things.

Where the river flowed out of the jungle into the sea we entered a world ablaze with light, suddenly vast and blue with the breadth of the sea and the sky and trimmed with shining beaches where men were making fishing-nets and repairing old canoes. We swam in the surf with a rabble of laughing young-sters, then sat on the sands in the heat of the sun, washed by a gentle breeze, carefully picking fleas from each other's hair. Later some friendly soul led us along a coastal shelf, skirting the edge of the swamps, to a thin little jungle trail which was only a faint depression winding over dark leaf-mould; and within an hour we found the coast besieged by swamps again.

Sometimes we wandered uncertainly through dripping jungle, or on beaches, clawing our way over rocks and muddy depths at river mouths where the drains of the flooded lowlands ripped into the sea in hissing, swirling conflict with the tide.

There were villages in the north, and charming avenues of palms and mangoes and hedges of hibiscus led the last few miles to Coco Beach. We walked barefoot along the sands towards the broad indented mouth of the Muni River; Moslem traders greeted us and fisherfolk called after us, and Anna sang a happy song and gazed ahead beyond the river at the tumbled, jungled hills of Spanish Guinea.

The settlement of Coco Beach was a single house on a slope by the shore, lavishly endowed with gardens, and the Comman-dant was a large and laughing fellow called Monsieur Larrieux. He entertained us in his house, a fine big house well furnished with the tusks of elephants and the skins of animals, and furniture of heavy wine-blackwood. He rifled through our passports, while his wife brought drinks and ice, pausing to remark on the indignities attending modern travel.

"You are not missionaries?" he inquired.

"No, we are students of ... of ..."

"Of anthropology," said Anna, who knew the word in French. "We measure the heads and bones of native people."

He chuckled. "That must be amusing; I wonder what the natives think?" Several days before, just to see what would happen, we had made friends with a native lad and solemnly proceeded to measure his head with a piece of string, discussing what kind of things might lie inside. But he was filled with pagan fears, uncertain what we were and if we coveted his skull: he commenced to tremble like a monkey newly caught, and gave little moans of terror, then suddenly dashed off up the beach, and we did not see him again.

"How did you come from Libreville?" asked Larrieux.

"Along the coast, on foot."

He glanced at us curiously, and silently sipped his drink.

"You are not students of anthropology," he said at length, "and you did not walk up the coast. But I am not concerned with what you are or how you came, I am only concerned with what you want to smuggle."

Ye gods, what next?

"Must we be smugglers? Could we not be students, or bird-watchers, or nothing at all?"

"What have you brought?" he asked abruptly.

"Nothing to smuggle, Commandant."

He shrugged. "Everyone who comes here smuggles something. The River Muni and everyone here thrives on contraband. The Spanish, the natives, the traders who come by sea; anything bought in Spanish Guinea brings twice the value here, and there's a nice rate of exchange for French currency in Bata. Are you sure you have nothing to smuggle?"

Curse the man: did he want to search us?

"Two dead fish," said Anna. "Some mangoes, a —"

"Nothing," I said firmly. "Nothing at all."

He wagged his head in disapproval. "Then I must give you something." He reached into his cabinet and brought forth a bottle of Ricard. "It is a tradition that no one comes here without smuggling some little thing," he explained. "You must take this, and smuggle it into Spanish Guinea. I forbid you to drink it before you arrive. Ah … you have visas for Spanish Guinea, of course? I did not notice them."

"Of course," she said quickly. He knew very well we had none.

"Then it will not be necessary for you to go directly to the Spanish frontier-post at Kogo … in fact that way might prove difficult, *non*? I will send you in my launch to Finca de Calatrava, a plantation about ten miles across the bay, and from there you can walk up the coast. It is not a difficult coast."

Here was the French Commandant deliberately showing us the way to circumvent the Spanish border control! I raised my glass to him in toast.

"Monsieur: an officer and a gentleman!"

He also raised his glass.

"*A bas les pics*!" Down with cops!

A mestizo trader came with us in the launch, bearing mysterious bundles which he guarded with close concern, north across the Franco-Spanish frontier in midstream. Up-river were tremendous swamps, out to sea was Corisco Island, a diminutive tropical paradise where the sands are as yellow as fine gold and pretty maidens sigh for men; it is known to Spanish traders as the Island of Love.

Finca de Calatrava was two houses set above a rocky shore amid rough slopes of Liberia coffee, a coarse grade of berry used for lending bulk to quality; and Señor de Portofax Doria became our host. He had business with the trader and his bundles, and when they were not looking we took the opportunity to stamp our passports with a rubber stamp we found. This was no border station, and Doria did not question our arrival; but the rubber stamp was an impressive seal which bore the legend "*Obras Publicas, Senales Maritimas, Caladtrava-Kogo*" and a coat of arms as well. We had by-passed the frontier control at Kogo, but such a fine and official-looking stamp might serve to further confuse the confusion which doubtless lay ahead.

The trader led us inland through jungle for some miles along a pleasant trail which wound among low hills, and a tempest came. A breath of wind sighed overhead, and scattered leaves fell gently on the trail; the tops of trees began to move with restless flutterings, we smelt the sweet new smell of approaching rain, and eddies of cool air drifted down from the jungle roof. Swollen clouds were racing overhead, darkly purple, drawing across the heavens like a blind and shrouding the coast with oppressive shadow. Our trader became nervous, and urged us to greater speed; thunder rattled across the sky, lightning stabbed the wilds and flickered among the clouds. A heavy gust of wind sheered over the jungle roof, tossing the upper branches and sending down leaves in showers. A stronger gust snapped twigs and rotten branches, then suddenly an air-quake was rushing across our heads, stripping branches, bending trees, thrashing the forest until it moaned, till all the jungle was moving and the vines were swaying, great lianas swinging to and fro, and debris was falling like confetti at Gretna Green.

The rain burst on us in a hissing fury, hard-driven by the gale, sheeting in a deluge on the trees above and pouring fast and faster all about us. It formed a thousand little rivulets that emptied on the trail and turned it to a shallow, swilling stream.

The trader was beckoning. He shouted, but we could not hear his voice. He plunged off up the trail as fast as he could run, and half wild with the splendour of the storm we followed after. Within a quarter of a mile we found him by a river, wrestling with a great canoe lodged in muddy shallows, and helped by several natives. God help us, no wonder he had wanted us to hurry! We must travel by the river, and it would be a raging sea within ten minutes: it was flowing like a mill-race now. We ran to his assistance; bags and bundles were flung aboard and everyone seized paddles and jumped in.

The river was only twenty yards in breadth, snagged with logs and sudden trees and thick low-hanging branches. The great canoe swung slowly out and gradually responded in the racing midstream current ... gathered speed ... faster, faster, there could be no stopping now, it was hell-bent for the coast or quick disaster. We paddled to gain surface speed and steer away from snags, but the canoe was long and broad and had its way.

Branches slapped and tore at us, thorn-vines clutched and hooked at us, rocks and tree-trunks missed the craft by inches. Blinding rain streamed down our faces, sudden humps and billows in the water sent us lurching wildly left and right, lifting, rolling, plunging through white rapids which invaded the canoe, by great bamboos and jungle true, and wicked snares of mangroves.

Streams cascaded into the river on either side; the current was growing stronger, goaded by the storm, and we fought to keep the craft from veering sideways on to snags, paddling and bailing and squinting through the rain at half-seen hazards.

Then we crashed headlong on a hidden rock. The bows shot high out of the water, and for a moment the canoe was almost airborne. Everything plunged downwards, there was a jarring crash, I was standing on my shoulders in the bilge, men were yelling. Water gushed aboard in one great wave, everything was upside down. Anna was shouting. The world was a rain-blurred vortex of rapid trees and plunging movement. A native was lying over the stern with his feet hooked round a seat, his body trailing in the water, grimly hanging on to the half-drowned trader, who had fallen in the river.

The canoe was almost foundering, but there were calmer waters now; the sea was close at hand, and ahead on a bend of the river was a logging settlement. The craft was manoeuvred inshore, the trader pulled aboard; he was pale, and sick, but quite alive.

SPANISH GUINEA

The coast of Spanish Guinea was a thousand shining beaches swept by sudden tempests and awash with creaming surf. It was a pageant of primitive splendour slowly unfolding through long days afoot, of Atlantic rollers thundering in white majesty over ragged reefs, of blossoming flamboyants mirrored red in emerald lagoons and dripping blooms among the hyacinths; a tasselled fringe of colour on the edge of Africa, ablaze with the strong sun and studded with small villages embedded in the jungle. The jungle was tall and deep, cut by numerous rivers and streams plumed with feathery palms which leant out over the dazzling sands and patterned them with shadows.

Each day was a leisurely idyll of small adventures and new friendships in new and pleasant places; sometimes we slept on the beach, sometimes in village huts; we went fishing on the sea and hunted crabs in rivers, and shoals of delighted youngsters taught us how to ride their frail canoes through heavy surf.

Policemen were about, so we could not linger long. Each large village had policemen who came to question us, frowning at Doria's stamp but ardently suspicious to find two stray foreigners walking on the beach. We spoke no Spanish, and they spoke nothing else. Twice we were arrested in logging settlements, and twice good fortune aided our escape; at Rio Benito, a prosperous town in deep domestic jungle at the mouth of a large river, two policemen and a soldier arrested us at night.

They had found us sitting by a fire among great logs half buried on the mud, finishing a meal of fish and plantains, and demanded with insistence that we go with them to see the Commandant. The soldier threatened with his rifle, but he had no bullets, so we walked with them until we came upon a church ablaze with lights and loud with lusty singing, and then Anna said, "I think we must go and pray. I think we need some prayer; and maybe we can lose ourselves here."

Churches are the traditional refuge of the poor and the persecuted, so against all opposition we marched into the church and walked along the aisle glancing to left and right as if for room; our enemies lingered uncertainly at the door. The congregation filled the building, standing on either side of us singing a warlike hymn with admirable zeal: but the preacher in his pulpit, baying at the ceiling and thrashing the air with a cane, caught sight of us and stared in disbelief, and faltered to a halt.

A woman in shorts, in church! Carrying luggage ... and a Beard in female dress!

It was too much. He gripped the sides of the pulpit and glared at us in mounting wrath. The hymn began to waver as the voices of those behind us faded and fell. Heads began to turn. Women gasped, and a thin murmur of excitement stirred behind us. We hurried up the last of the aisle, darted out of a side door, cantered away in the night and crossed the river in a stolen canoe.

We fared on up the coast more rapidly, and came to Bata.

André glanced towards the door and lowered his voice. "It is a bad place, this Spanish Guinea. It is very hard for black men, not like on the French side. If a black man steals he is flogged till he is nearly dead; if he steals again he is tortured. If he makes some honest money he must keep silent, otherwise he will be arrested every week and will have to pay bribes to the police until he has no more money, and then he may go to prison. There is a big prison, and it is always full; and when it is too full some are sent off to an island."

"Slaves," said the Muni man. "We are all slaves."

"The Spaniards worship a woman; the black men have no position at all unless they worship the woman too. They have no —" The breath hissed sharply through his teeth and he stared towards the door. "Except the African police," he whispered. "They are the worst of all. Look!"

The two policemen with the rifles were entering the room, and conversation had ebbed abruptly to an expectant hush. One was a corporal, tall and glabrous black and thick of body; his face had a rough and ungainly cast well suited to the crooked sneer which curled his puffy lips. The policemen were clad in slovenly khaki shirts and shorts, soiled and limp with perspiration. The corporal had puttees bound about his legs, but the size of his horny feet denied the possibility of boots.

They came straight towards us, strolling with easy confidence and enjoying the latent drama of the scene, observing us with insolent amusement. They paused by our table, and the corporal hooked his thumb in the sling of his shouldered rifle while the smaller man stood grinning lewdly down at Anna. The corporal addressed me harshly in loud Spanish. André spoke to him, and turned to me. "Someone has told the Commandant you are here. You must report to him at nine o'clock in the morning."

The corporal helped himself to one of André's cigarettes and said something else, gazing hungrily at Anna's blouse. For various little reasons I decided I disliked him intensely.

"He says he must have your passports now."

"We will take them ourselves to the Commandant in the

morning. We do not carry them for the amusement of idle imbeciles."

André worriedly translated. A smouldering light appeared in the corporal's eyes, and he spat on the table-top with obscene deliberation before replying.

"He says he does not believe you have passports. He says it is forbidden for you to remain here. You must spend the night in the Guria Hotel."

The corporal leant forward and grasped our bottle; with abrupt passion I rose to my feet and swiped it from his hand. It cannoned against the wall and splintered to the floor with a tinkling splash of broken glass and wine. His face crinkled with hot anger, his lips quivered back from strong white teeth in an ugly snarl. In a vacuum of silence we stood glaring at each other from a distance of three feet, while passion ebbed to chill hostility.

"Tell him he was hatched in a *pissoir* drain," I snapped, forgetting Anna's presence, "and that we'll sleep where we damn please."

Harsh words were spoken on both sides, and by the time the two policemen left the bar was closed, the room was almost empty, and André was reduced to nervous stammering.

"You have p-papers? You have passports?"

"Papers and passports, yes," said Anna laconically, "but no visas."

"No visas? *Merde*! Did you p-pass the frontier control at Kogo?"

"We are smugglers, Monsieur André," she mocked him. "We do not pass by frontier controls."

"*Merde, m-merde*!" He squirmed in his chair. "It is bad enough to be a black man here without a visa — but, *Dieu*, for a white man to be here smuggling, with a lady, drinking with black men, and no visa! The Spaniards think evil of everyone, even each other, and here are two s-strangers, two *blancs*, who have come on foot, and avoided the border control, and abuse policemen … there are no consuls here. They will think you are C-Communists. You will be put in prison. You will be … be …"

"Eaten, probably," said Anna.

"Twenty years at Santa Isabel," mourned the Muni man.

"Could we not go away, now?" I suggested eagerly, with visions of us being pursued hot-foot along the beaches.

"They are waiting for you to do that!" André said excitedly. "They are outside now, the two *pics*, hoping you will try to run away. That they would love. That they hope for. Then you would be in p-prison tonight."

"We will be deported," said Anna smugly. "I have never been deported from a Spanish colony. British and French and almost Belgian, but never Spanish. Now it can happen. Where do you think they will send us? To a nice island?"

"One is deported to Spanish colonies, not from them," I reminded her testily.

"We must think of some interesting story."

One could be sure they would be interested in whatever story we chose to tell.

The Muni came with us in the morning; André was nowhere to be seen. Two *askaris* who had been stationed on either side of the building slouched along behind us as we climbed to the inland edge of the town, and Spaniards about their morning affairs observed us with candid curiosity. The Muni man murmured melancholy warnings beyond the *askaris'* hearing.

He led us to the inland side of town.

"The Commandant is a fierce man," he said. "Fierce and cruel, and very much respected. He is strong, and easily angry; you must be weak before him … the Contrôl Civil is built on the edge of the city, where the screams cannot be heard." He sighed gloomily, and pointed to a new cream building with blank brown shutters. "There it is. Men enter the door, and some never return. I will wait here, and pray."

Anna shuddered deliciously, and I suspected she was deriving some inverted form of amusement from our sorry plight. We entered the building, with the two *askaris* close behind us, and Spanish officials in the heady uniforms of Balkan princes eyed us somberly and ordered us to wait. Minutes passed. Sounds of shouting and hysterical excitement issued from a nearby office; the door swung abruptly open, an African was flung out, and a policeman of his own race helped him into the street with a powerful kick in his pants. The victim stumbled in the dust, then turned and grinned, danced a little jig, and went off laughing happily.

A moustachio'd rear-admiral magnificently clad in a white uniform studded with medals and mounted with fabulous epaulettes grunted to us, and jerked his thumb towards the office.

The Commandant, Señor Carmona, was a man of powerful frame running to thick flesh, seated heavily behind a polished desk like some atrabilious Buddha. His head was a shining oval, clean-shaven and completely bald; his jowls drooped, his eyes were small and hard and hooded under heavy brows, and he had withal the morose demeanour of some portly but embittered vulture brooding on a butcher's block. He ignored our greeting and snapped one word.

"Passports!"

We handed them across the desk. He had the coldly intransigent manner of a Gestapo chief, of someone accustomed to dealing impassively with other people's lives. No wonder the natives feared him; he looked like an arrogant bully accustomed to the harsh misuse of power; such men do not improve with age, for the wine of their life is sour, and he was already old. He belched and wiped his mouth, and scrutinised the passports with a practised eye; we noticed with grim amusement that the Calatrava stamps caused him some bewilderment. He stated firmly, in fair French, "You have no visas."

A story had been arranged. Anna leant lightly against the desk, and using all her persuasive wiles and feminine appeal she began, "Forgive us, *monsieur le commandant*, if we have caused you any trouble. We are students and have been trying to travel from Angola to the Cameroons. We —"

"Why do you have no visa?" he demanded brusquely.

She smiled, a little icily.

"We asked for visas for this country when we were in Luanda, but the Spanish Consul said he would have to send our application through Madrid." She had met Gestapo officials as a child, when she carried papers for the Underground from Amsterdam to Friesland, and had on all but one occasion convinced them of her innocence. "We had intended to take an inland road," she continued sweetly, "and he said the visas would be sent to the inland border to wait for us; but the road was washed away by floods, and we had to come up the coast."

Such was the story; and no one could prove it false without great trouble.

"You came up the coast? By ship?"

"Walking, *monsieur le commandant*. It was quite difficult." She smiled with the wistful courage of a hard-tried heroine. "It is nice to arrive in such a lovely colony as yours. Everyone is good to us in Spanish Guinea; we are too happy to be here."

Happy, the truthless vixen!

"You walked all the way?" He raised his eyes, and they flickered over us like the questing tongue of a serpent. He was suspicious.

"Our map is very small, *monsieur le commandant*, and it did not look so far."

He browsed through our passports for some minutes, sullen and unsmiling, pausing ever and anon to regard some item with shrewd interest. He inspected the manner in which the various passports were bound together, fingering the waxen seals, and then stared balefully at each of us in turn.

"Do you collect stamps?"

I hesitated uncertainly, and even Anna was puzzled. Was this some Spanish joke? Was he questioning our Calatrava stamp?

"I am a collector of foreign stamps," he went on. "You have some in your passports I have never seen before."

Sweet blue eyes: a dragon turned philatelist!

"We have other stamps," said Anna a little breathlessly. She was digging in her tattered wallet, tipping out scraps of paper, visiting-cards, addresses, photographs, wine-labels, stamps, odds and ends of nonsense which the Commandant considered with mild surprise. "Here are some stamps from South Africa, and Rhodesia. And Holland, and Angola."

She placed them in his hand and he examined them closely, one by one. Meanwhile I searched among papers and old letters in my pockets.

"I have only some from Australia," I apologised.

"Ah? Australia?"

He had not seen such stamps before, and fingered them with interest. A platypus had to be explained, as far as one might do so, and a plausible theory was invented for what seemed to be the likeness of a wooden lizard.

"May I keep them?" he asked politely.

"But of course, *mon commandant*, with great pleasure." He could eat them if he wished. Surely he would not ask us for foreign stamps and then put us in a cell? He rang a desk-bell, and gave orders to an aide. The aide went away and returned with two other men, and the three of them began turning out drawers and cabinets to hunt for stamps. They tore them off envelopes and snipped them from documents, and soon the desk was littered with stamps from half a dozen Spanish colonies.

"You must take these," he said, pushing them towards us. "Ah — I will give you the current series of Guinea Española."

He presented us with two sets of new stamps to the total value of more than thirty shillings, then smiled quizzically and said, "I had almost forgotten why you are here. You say you wish to go to the Cameroons?"

"Er ... *oui, mon commandant*."

Gods, we were alive, we were free!

"Walking, I suppose." He took two large black-and-white stamps and fixed one in each of our passports, then added two fine rubber stamps and scrawled something to the effect that we were permitted to leave the country, at once, on the route to the Cameroons.

Anna smiled a little wistfully.

"Are we not to be deported, Commandant?"

"Young woman," he said firmly, "you are at this very moment being deported." He glanced at his watch. "It is now three minutes before ten o'clock. You are permitted to remain in the city for one hour and three minutes; at the end of one hour and four minutes you must be gone. And north, no other way."

"*Oui, monsieur le commandant*." She gave him a dazzling smile.

"I warn you that if you do not leave Bata in that time, and do not go north, you will be formally arrested, charged with illegal entry to the colony, and you will be put in prison. I assure you."

"*Oui, monsieur le commandant*." She was trying not to laugh, and her smile was infectious.

"You must pay me one and a half pesetas each," he murmured soberly. "For the exit permits."

Threepence each; it did not seem too much for the price of freedom.

CAMEROONS ▬▬▬▬▬

We had no visas for the Cameroons.

"It's on again," I muttered. "No visas, and no place else to go."

Well, it did not seem to matter any more. Doubtless we would be deported to the next colony, and to the one after that, and so on until we had travelled right round the coast of Africa and it began all over again. It was like playing chess with a poker-machine inhabited by jumping-beans: logic rode the chips of happenchance.

"We can use our Equatorial Africa visas again," said Anna impassively. "The Cameroons are really part of the same territory, and maybe a visa good for one is good for both."

"We've used them twice already. They were valid for ten days, and now they're so old the ink is beginning to fade."

"If we used them twice already we can use them three times," she argued determinedly. "There are so many stamps all over the place no one will notice they've been used even once. And does it matter if they do? We can be deported to another place. They cannot send us back, I hope, so they must send us farther north. What is north?"

"Sand, eventually. I once heard of a man who was shunted back and forth between Syria and Iraq for three months. He had no visas for either place. He died, or went mad; I forget."

The canoe was propelled by paddles shaped like broad-bladed spears, and the crew were singing a low and throaty song. The edge of the sea was black with the discharge of the river, and rollers were snowing over reefs beyond the point.

"We could have sneaked up the coast by canoe from London village."

"And give some cretin of a gendarme half a thousand francs?" she flared. "I will give policemen nothing but sharp teeth!"

French *askaris* escorted us through the jungle on a narrow road to the house of the French commandant, which stood on a pleasant hill above the sea. This commandant was a dark little man, unshaven and ill-clad, and when we arrived he was adzing a long okume log to the shape of a canoe. He stared at us with blank appraisal for a moment as we approached, then spat contemptuously and continued with his work. The *askaris* saluted, thudding their bare heels on the ground, and without even raising his head he told them to go away.

His shirt hung loosely outside his trousers, his sandals were unlaced; one might have taken him for some hispid beachcomber, and for a long time he ignored us, until Anna seated herself on the half-shaped log, not a foot from his flashing adze, and began to roll a cigarette with casual indifference to his angry pause. She licked the paper delicately and lit the cigarette, then glanced pensively down at the log and slowly wagged her head in disapproval. The Commandant's brows climbed his forehead in surprise. I checked an impulse to laugh, and taking a fishing-line from my pocket began to measure the width and length of the log, and then the height, while he looked on with frank inquiry.

Anna and I looked sadly at each other. We pursed our lips and shook our heads, and the Commandant went to the head of the log and squinted down its length.

"Is it no good?" he asked.

"It is no good."

"Too long," said Anna.

"Too wide."

"Crooked, too."

"And rather thin."

"When it was a tree it was much better," she observed.

"But it is a fine log," he protested. "I had it specially brought from the Spanish side."

I walked round it, carefully studying the sides, and murmured dismally, "It doesn't have one. It cannot stay."

"What?"

"Perhaps it's underneath," said Anna hopefully.

"I doubt it. They never are."

"What is underneath?" demanded the Commandant, squatting on his heels to look.

"The visa. It is a Spanish log and it has no visa. You must deport it."

A thin little smile twitched at his lips, and he began to chuckle.

"Come into the house," he said. "You have the madness too. We will take some medicine."

LIBERIA

Beyond the Mani River lay the land of demons, thieves, and Leopard men; "the most beautiful place in all the world, where all men love each other and are happy."

Over the bridge and round a bend a sentry lay snoring damply in a hammock by the road; a rifle lay below him on the ground, and a handkerchief covering his face gently rippled as he breathed. This, then, was the first Liberian, who might change into a leopard or produce a cup of tea; yet sentries are commonly tutored to suspicion, and it might have been wise to slip past silently, but the slight sounds of my passing caught his ear. A gust of breath blew the cloth from his face, and he turned his head to fix me with his glittering black eyes.

"Hey, you!"

He sat upright, and groped for his rifle with his toes. His voice was harsh with a hint of arrogance.

"Weh you goin', whi'-man?"

"Well, Monrovia," I suggested in apologetic terms. Monrovia was two hundred miles away, and an African might be forgiven for doubting that any European would journey there on foot. His gaze moved slowly over me with a vaguely puzzled air.

"Weh my dash?"*

"I have no dash, brother. Where my tea?"

"Erry man cross tha' bridge mus' pay dash. Gi' me money, whi'-man!"

"You think I'm a fool to walk on foot with money in my

* tip, bribe

pocket? I have no money. No-momma-no-poppa-no-whisky-no-cig'rette."

"You goh no money? How you eat foo', whi'-man? You scratch onna ground like chicken? If you goh no money for dash they put you inside, quick."

He considered the point for a moment, and then chuckled and said, not unkindly, "Okay, whi'-man; start walkin'. Git, onetime!"*

Beyond a patch of swamp, on the brow of a gentle hill, was a ragged town called Ganta, a sprawling village of adobe and thatch and corrugated iron etched with erosion and stained with neglect, a sad town, unkempt as a lion too long in its cage, and shorn of its pride by the shabby edge of gimcrack western commerce. Children came to greet me, half a dozen laughing youngsters who scampered about the road shouting foolish things in broken English, no doubt pretending this white stranger was some terrible forest monster, and playfully tossing stones; but when a pebble struck my brow they ran off up the hill, delighted and alarmed and shrill as a flight of starlings, and a drop of blood trickled from my eye.

The road to the coast swung right, through a litter of untidy huts and wilting wooden stores; to the left was Eleanor's Beer Parlour, a whitewashed tavern daubed with crayon drawings like some child's interpretation of a dream, and beyond was a small mud hut which housed the Frontier Control. Three soldiers of the Liberian Frontier Force lounged in the shade in hammocks, apparently exhausted; two monkeys, freshly caught, were hanging by their paws from a line between two huts, one of them quite dead and the other whimpering piteously like a baby, and feebly struggling, while the Customs officer squatted on the threshold of his office bruising it with pebbles from a catapult. The flag of Liberia drooped from a wooden pole, a star and eleven stripes; the town was half asleep in the noonday sun.

The Customs officer was a toadlike individual, intensely black, his face was seamed with thin tattoos and a pendulous lower lip weighed down his open mouth. He paused in his play to observe my approach with critical inquiry, and fitting another

* quick

pebble to his catapult he demanded, "Who you, whi'-man? Wha'
you want?"

He rose reluctantly to his feet, accepted the proffered passport,
and listened to a sketchy explanation while his lip fell lower, and
lower, and threatened to turn completely inside out. The soldiers
were awake, and staring from their hammocks with neutral
curiosity.

"You mean you walkin'?" protested the Lip. "You goh no
car? Whi'-man, you crazy!" He shrugged, as if to dismiss a
worthless riddle. "You mus' pay two'n'ha'dollar. And gi' me
that bread you got."

"Two and a half dollars? For what?"

"Fo' visa, whi'-man."

"But pardon me, I have a visa in my pass—"

"Whi-man, errybody come in this country mus' pay two'n ha'
dollar. Errybody. I got orders. Don' mind if you goh one, two,
three visas, now you buy another. Erry man come here mus' pay
two'n'ha dollar. You wan' come here, you mus' pay two'n ha'
dollar. You got two'n ha' dollar?"

"No."

"Okay, you don' come here. You get the hell out. Okay?
Reg'lation says if man come here don' have money for feed
himself, he mus' get the hell out. If you don' have money for pay
me, then you don' have money for feed yourself, and you get the
hell out. Why you wan' come here, whi'-man? You godly-godly
man?"

A pox on the fool: I must bribe him or be turned back, and the
bribe would take my last Gold Coast pound. There was a visa in
the passport, and important documents had been signed declaring that I would not break the law, sabotage the peace, or
overthrow the government by violence, but that meant nothing
to this frogling. Mustering such dignity as a purseless traveller
might I addressed him firmly in pious tones.

"I am a man of God. God is my guardian and travels at my
side: and woe unto him who seeks to bar my path. Do you not
read your Bible? 'Let prostitutes and passport officers heed the
word of the Lord, lest they seek the purse of the righteous, for
the harlots shall drink of the poison-cup, and the Lord shall turn
the officers to eunuchs.' Saint Paul to the Philistines. Do you

seek to hinder the work of the Lord? Would you risk being turned to a eunuch?"

He was unmoved. He spat on the floor, and said, "Two 'n ha' dollar. Even godly-godly men mus' pay. Give or git, onetime!"

Infidel! Dung of a viper!

"If you is godly-godly man, you go see Dr Harley. He mission man, he give you two'n ha' dollar. When you gi' me two'n ha' dollar, you go Monrovia. You can take God too, no charge for Him."

Blasphemer! These people were barbarians. Well, I would go to the mission, and see this Dr Harley; he could change my pound, if nothing else; this fiend was only interested in pocketing two and a half dollars for his personal gain.

"All right, I'll go and see this man. But I must give him dash, if he is to help me. You give me that monkey, the live one, and I'll give it to Harley for dash."

He was tempted by the cash return in prospect, and I went off to the mission with the monkey. It fought against its bonds, whimpering and biting, bruised and bleeding from the pebbles and hard knocks: when loosed on the edge of the jungle it stood quivering with fear, then limped into the undergrowth and disappeared.

∿∿∿∿∿

MONROVIA

Tony wagged his head. "Someone should stay here long enough to write a book on Monrovia."

Here was the answer!

"I have to go and see the President. Can you lend me a suit?"

"Why, sure. The Old Man'll be glad to see you. Er, what?"

"I think I'm going to write a book. A book on Liberian legends and tribal folk-tales. And he's going to commission me to do it, and pay for it, maybe."

He regarded me with a droll amusement.

"Could you write a book?"

"Any fool can write a book if he's sufficiently hard pressed. But I'll need a suit to see the Old Man, and references too."

"Well, it's a good idea to see him, anyway," he said with cautious sympathy. He scratched his nose, and added hopefully. "He gave a prostitute fifty dollars once, to help her start a decent life; he'd give turkey to a yellow dog."

"Indeed."

"But you might find it difficult to see him; he's surrounded by bum politicians who don't like whites."

Fifteen days passed by, long days of vain endeavour frought with intrigue with high officials, laced with promises which fell from politicians' lips like honey from a poisoned hive, before a Russian refugee arranged an interview.

The Big Man's office, in the Executive Mansion, had the sombre and intimate atmosphere of some pundit's sanctuary; President Tubman himself was a thickset gentleman of nigh sixty years, with coarse but kindly countenance, and he sat behind a table of polished mahogany littered with papers and bound documents. His confident and unassuming manner marked him as a man of unaffected self-possession. A practical man: he had built himself a palace in the country, and his only opposition had seen fit to quit the country on a fast, unscheduled plane.

The Big Man's casual gaze was sharp with shrewd appraisal.

"We have a few minutes. Glad you came."

His eyes were twinkling as he reached forward to shake my offered hand and click fingers, and I wondered if my mission was already a public jest. Tony's fine suit looked well enough: but had he remarked me loitering through the streets wearing dusty trousers and old shoes, and a limp straw hat with two great holes in it? He bade me to take an armchair at his side, and I set my borrowed briefcase on the floor.

"I read your letter," he said. "Interesting idea. Cigar?"

Of course: it was not often one had the chance to smoke cigars with presidents. The letter had said much, but some additional spiel seemed required.

"Mr President, you've got a magnificent treasury of folklore in this republic, and it's the greatest cultural asset you could wish for. Songs, ballads, tribal legends: they form a vast unwritten literature, the refined wit and wisdom of old men handed down by word of mouth for centuries — but once they're lost, forgotten, no power on earth can bring them back. It's high time a museum was made for them. The past is easily forgotten, if it is not written down; and these legends must be preserved, Mr President."

"What exactly is your proposition?" he asked bluntly. Dipping into the briefcase I produced a contract and handed it to him, and he rapidly scanned the two typewritten pages. The contract was conveniently vague but concerned a proposed book of selected folk-tales from Liberian tribes; the work to be "officially assisted" and to become the property of the Liberian Government, if judged worthy, on payment of a suitable fee.

"Interesting," he admitted guardedly. 'I've been trying to get the Bureau of Folkways to do this for two years, but, h'm, they … and you say you can do it in three months?"

It was said the President had witnessed the Grebo-Bassa fight forty years before, when his own uncle was killed and eaten. He glanced down at the contract.

"Mr Simonovitch says you've done similar work before."

A small sheaf of references was passed to him. They had been carefully edited and could not easily be discredited, and proclaimed this penniless poseur to be an expert on ethnology and the author of several fictitious works on folklore.

"H'm … well, these seem to the point. How much do you have in mind as reimbursement for your efforts?"

Ah so? Was he asking how much money I would want? The fee? Figures scuttled about my mind and dollars fluttered through the air like driven snow. The Russian had warned me to keep the figure low: but if the price named was too high, why, then one could name a lower one. I inspected my cigar, and declared with feverish indifference, "A thousand dollars, Mr President."

There, it was done! He would have me thrown out, pilloried in a public place, hounded from the land. An impostor, a fool, a vagabond at large in the streets of Monrovia, demanding a thousand dollars for some arrant piece of nonsense!

"A thousand dollars?" he echoed mildly. So? But he was not dismayed. He even sounded interested, to a small degree. Would he bargain, then? Eight hundred, six hundred, five. Why, he might pay something: the idea, after all, was not so bad. He puffed at his cigar, and demanded calmly, "Do you think a thousand dollars is enough?"

Enough? Enough, by the gods, when I had not a paper centime in my pockets and lived on charity? Sarcastic villain! But one could bargain with him.

"I think," he said slowly, with the shadow of a smile, "I think we'd better make it two thousand. One thousand is an honest offer, but you will have expenses. One thousand dollars now, and one thousand when, and if, the Government decides to buy the book."

I floated out of the Mansion with a thousand dollars burning in my pocket, and bought rich clothes, as a rich man should, and plunged into the city's social round.

∧∧∧∧∧∧∧

The urgent notes of a bugle spilled out abruptly over the hills, and a volley of rifle-fire sent startled echoes flying through the jungle. The village of Bellefani, deep in the hinterland, was aflame with festival and feasting and the throb of fifty drums, swirling with excited dancing girls and vivid with the finery of paramount chiefs and princes: tribal deputations in ceremonial robes had been pouring in for days from the mountains and the plains, until this humble roadhead village looked like the centre of some kingly pilgrimage.

The President was travelling through the provinces on tour, and his passage was attended by spectacular rejoicing such as rarely is accorded any man. Chiefs came bearing tribute, commissioners to pay homage, dancing girls and drummers converged along the route: and now this feast was over and a three days' trek north-west to distant Voinjama began — by jungle trails and mountain fastnesses, to the most remote corner of the land.

Hammock-bearers were assembled, blood and palm-wine were spilt on the trail to invoke the goodwill of the gods and satisfy the appetites of evil forest spirits; a military band struck up a stirring air and swung forward into the jungle flanked by standard-bearers and soldiers armed as if for war. Thirty hammocks followed after, gently swaying from the shoulders of bull-muscled tribesmen, with the Big Man's royal litter in the lead; behind him, hammock-borne, were five generals and the Vice-President, ministers, and senators of the Executive Council, and a single but elated European. A hundred hand-picked porters, a company of soldiers, a hundred and fifty hammock-bearers: a fine procession for the hinterland to see!

Every village was appraised of the President's approach by the bugle's strident peals; drummers and musicians and dancers would join the column for a time and fall away, groups of men and women sang and chanted as we passed, and the way was looped with tall triumphal arches made from jungle blooms and palms.

It was a wild and fascinating land, an uncharted wilderness of crumpled hills and rivers spanned by swinging bridges, tangled with quick streams cascading through ravines and densely packed with the tall mossed timbers of the rain-forests: here the mountains divided the rains, sending half of them south to the Atlantic and the other half north in a thousand streams and cataracts to form the Niger River. It was a land which brooded damply under the lash of violent storms, the home of the Thunderbeast and the Sky-god and countless evil monsters; secret societies held mysterious rituals and made sacrifice by the light of the moon, and the dread Lausing stalked the jungles, hideous and cruel, with bleeding talons, seizing maidens. Only the Wurri and the Wuuni, those indomitable little demon-eaters, disguised as something like a cat but the scourge of all walking evil, saved the tribes from being utterly overcome by terrible Things.

Superstitious traditions spread a mantle of fear across the hills. Following the recurrent disintegration of the Sudan empires during a thousand years and more, warrior tribes had come down south in search of the sea and its salt, or better land. They hacked and slashed their way through settled tribes, invading the coastal forests with blood on their spears and the lust for land deep-rooted in their hearts: and beyond the mountains of the Niger watershed they killed the "little, hairy men" and settled on the coast.

The tribes which followed in invading waves pressed hard against the first, and finally settled among the hills and mountains. They brought with them their heathen rites and worship of inanimate things, their strange superstitions, and black magic; they brought, too, their hunger for war and bloody opportunism, and feuded bitterly among themselves until, twenty and thirty years ago, the Government's militant persuasion brought uneasy peace.

Here was the President of the nation showing the flag, counting heads, requiring tribute from the chiefs and a reckoning with commissioners; and if his welcome was invariably one of obeisance and homage, it was not for nothing that a hundred well-armed troops marched with the column.

And, by the devil's tail, it was a fine and splendid thing to travel in such style, gently swinging in a hammock borne by slaves! Here was a noble enterprise for any vagabond: to travel, and sleep, and sup with the presidential suite, a single European among these Negro lords, to be carried by sweating serfs down valley slopes and over rivers and up great mountainsides, with flags flying and the bugle flaring wildly, and drummers pounding salute and maidens casting flowers, and dancing almost naked for one's pleasure: here was a fine adventure for any fool! Here was a page of ancient splendour, moving in pomp among these pagan tribes, among these swarming mountains which hid their diamonds and their gold. Why, we were some Ptolemaic caravan, breasting the Nile jungles with gold and frankincense on pilgrimage to Egypt's shrines. We were Hannibal's conquering vanguard, or a cavalcade of Persians following the old Silk Road from Mesopotamia to far Cathay, or Spanish *conquistadores* marching through Panama, laden with loot and bullion, to the sea!

A leisurely signal, and a bearer would bring brandy in a flask; a dollar or two well spent had anticipated the rigours of the journey. One long burning draught, and then another, and the bottle passed among the sweating porters.

"Hurry, slaves! Faster, faster!"

FRENCH WEST AFRICA ▰▰▰

Bamako is a Sudanese city set hard by the Niger, a splendid riverside metropolis flanked by adobe slums and orchard-forests, sprawling in a valley between tall ramparts of black rock.

While wandering through the city seeking pleasure I chanced upon the Arab called Akbou.* He was sitting by a gutter in earnest conversation with some scoundrel when he saw me at a distance, and within a second only the glimpse of a long grey robe disappearing in a mango-tree, followed by the astonished scoundrel's gaze, was evidence that he had been there at all. Approaching the scoundrel, a dog-faced wretch in rags, unwashed, with stable filth in his dank black locks and the dung of moths in his beard, I saluted him agreeably and said, "Pardon, I seek a man called Akbou, an Arab horse-thief. Have you seen him?"

He shrugged, and sneered aggressively, and answered, "He is not here, white man. Find him somewhere else."

Silver coins glittered in my hand.

"Men say he is your friend. I wish to cut his throat, and I have … seven hundred francs to help me find him."

I fingered a thin dagger, and his eyes grew wide with wonder. From the corner of my eye I could see my shoes, on Akbou's feet, perched on a branch of the mango-trees. The scoundrel quickly rubbed his nose, with his gaze fixed on the coins, and withdrew a little from the tree with one hand outstretched.

"Akbou is in the tree, patron, above your head!"

I gave him the money and looked up into the tree, laughing.

"Ho, Akbou! Such fine friends you have — this miserable Judas reckons to sell your throat for seven silver pieces. Hey? Talk to him. Tell him something!"

The discomfited shoe-thief came down from the tree, and I noticed that the shoes had served him well: they had been shod with tyre-rubber of a certain famous brand, so that as he walked on a sandy road they printed "nilehciM, nilehciM, nilehciM" on the sand.

"Salaam, my friend," he said, grinning brazenly, a tall and kingly felon.

* Akbou had stolen Pinney's shoes some months before, on the Ivory Coast.

"Salaam indeed. Did you go to Dakar?"

"No, friend. I had trouble in Kankan."

"You were in prison, I hope?"

But he was silent; he stared down at his shoes — surely they were his by now — and hurriedly glanced away.

"I am going to Dakar tomorrow on the train," I continued. "First class."

"To Dakar? First class? But it is costly!"

"I hve enough money to buy the train, if I wish. You should have come to Liberia: a man can sweep up dollars in the gutter with a broom. Are you staying in Bamako?"

"I would go to Gao, good friend, but I am a poor man."

"Gao? What is there at Gao?"

A convention of shoe-thieves, no doubt.

"Patron, there is everything at Gao," he said, and a hopeful glint had entered his eyes. "It is a city of dancing-girls and music, and sweet herbs by the river. It is one of the twelve doors to paradise. And Gao is holy. Three visits to the Shrine of Kings is equal to one pilgrimage to Mecca, and this will be my third, with Allah's help."

"But Allah's help is not enough, that you stay here?" This place Gao might hold some interest. Sweet herbs, forsooth!

"One needs money to purchase the help of Allah, my friend."

Devil, here was an infidel! From Gao a road led north across the desert, as I knew; music, and sweet herbs and dancing-girls in Gao, and then north to Europe for the spring ... we would discuss this thing. And if we were to go to Gao, why, then we would go.

Taxi-drivers were consulted and one was found who, for a reasonable price, would take us seven hundred miles north-east to Gao, the gate of paradise; fifty dollars to be paid in advance. Akbou's scoundrel came with us, for no apparent reason; and sacks of kola-nuts for trade, doubtless bought with Allah's help, were pressed into the boot, and greasy sacks of oddments were piled upon the roof.

From the rich green wealth of Bamako the road snaked out into the desolate Sudan, the semi-desert, through barren wastes of sand and fragrant thornbush forests, a Biblical wilderness of sheep and cows and wooden ploughs where life had never risen above primitive simplicity. But he who travels fast, skimming the face of the land at speed, remains indeed a stranger to the land; and when I would alight, or tarry here, or there, my companions cried out for haste.

"They are nothing, these people," Akbou explained. "They are poor, they have nothing, no learning, no books; if you walk among them they may rob you. Let us go on to Gao, patron: soon you will be in paradise."

Indeed, certain signs suggested that the road might end abruptly at the gates of either paradise or hell: for during a day and a night, and this second morning, my two companions and the driver had been in furtive conversation. Akbou and the scoundrel sat behind me, and each of them had a dagger; it was a lonely road, and the single thrust of a knife would earn them the roll of dollars I possessed. Aye, it is not well to fare abroad in foreign lands with riches; or, if with riches, to travel with knaves and rogues; and the sly glances and innuendoes, and guttural mutterings in Arabic, pricked imagination with misgivings. Akbou had stolen my wallet when it was empty: why should he not do so now that it was full? And how auspicious would be his pilgrimage, if made with the help of Allah wrested from an Unbeliever!

And what madness had possessed me, to hurry like a fugitive past these quaint cubistic villages and the smiling men and women who waved gaily as we passed? A fool's folly, to be sure; the joy of travelling is rather in the journey, than the goal.

So it was that when we came upon a small group of musicians walking north along the road I asked the driver to stop the taxi, and he did. But when I had alighted I turned to Akbou, saying, "I leave you here. Goodbye."

"What?" He was incredulous, and utterly dismayed. "You cannot leave, patron: we have only come half-way."

"And half-way is paid for. Go now on your own. I will walk."

"But patron ... *we* cannot go, my friend, if you do not. Who will pay?"

"Allah perhaps, or your sacks of kola-nuts. Forgive me, I do not trust your knives. Good-bye."

As I walked away the three men emerged from the car and strode after me, and fearful of their purpose I ran. They ran after me, crying out in protest. The musicians observed this sudden cavalcade descending upon their rear and they, too, became alarmed and sought refuge in quick flight; so that four bewildered minstrels went galloping up the road with fear clawing at their heels, a nervous European scudded rapidly after them, and three Arabs bounded along behind shouting curses.

Fear lends a fugitive the speed of the sudden bat: the Arabs fell behind, and I pursued the dismayed musicians into a waste of thorn on a narrow track; but when they saw I was but one they paused, and warily returned my greeting. They were dapper young Malinke men clad in robes of scarlet and white, and red turbans, like court jesters, and they carried three xylophones and a set of drums and a sort of mandolin. We had no common language, but after much discussion I gave them coins, demanding music, and we walked and jigged for several miles, playing music until we came to Mopti on the Niger.

Beyond the river the sun was sinking into the barren plains, scattering topaz on the river and burnishing the town with orange light. Every alley and courtyard was set for opera, deep in shadow but quick with movement of cloaked and turbaned figures and flickering lamps: the oil-wicks of street stalls threw moving light on leaning walls, shone fleetingly on swarthy faces and coloured robes, an ivory bracelet, a silver dagger, white teeth and laughing eyes above a heavy golden necklace ... the ruddy flare of wayside kitchens splintered the gloom with shafts of glowing yellow snared by spiralling webs of steam, and the pungent smells of wood-smoke and smouldering incense pastilles wreathed about the passing throng as if careless temple acolytes paraded by an altar.

These were the Kardo people, the Bobo, and the Perl; fishermen and cattlemen, and warriors turned to trade. An ancient minaret loomed darkly in the gathering night, old men were seated before the mosque in idle conversation; hard by was a dance-hall where six young girls decked in gold and trinkets and little else danced with lewd abandon in the company of menfolk, selling a moment's pleasure to those who cared to bid. For a time we watched them, the Malinke men and I, then purchased fish and manioc and entered a baker's hut to buy flat bread.

"*Merde!*" said the baker. "What arrives? *Un blanc*?" His eyes popped, and he clasped his fat perspiring belly. "And music-men!" He stared at the food steaming gently in my hands, and laughter shook his paunch and quivered his fat shoulders. "And he has fish and manioc, and comes for bread ... Ho, Monsieur Blanc, make your slaves play music, and be welcome!"

And welcome we were; for when he found the *blanc* was not a Frenchman he led us to an inner courtyard and showed us rooms with mats where we might sleep, and when I gave him money he threw it in the street. He was from Senegal, and his name was Seaku San; a jolly rascal, rich with shining folds of flesh and gusts of rumbling laughter. When his favourite concubine came to the room where we squatted on rugs and cushions he drolly rolled his eyes and slapped his thighs.

"*Jolie, non*? You like her, Monsieur Blanc?"

She was attractive in her fashion, her face was pleasant and her body lithe and supple; her skin was nearly black, but smooth and shining like fine satin, and she moved with the leisurely grace of kelp on the tide. She wore her wealth upon her. A necklace of large amber balls glowed softly at her throat, and golden coins; splendid crescent wafers of worked gold, wide as a woman's hand, tinkled crisply at her ears, and amulets of ivory were on her arms, her hair was oiled and perfumed, and intricately plaited in a pattern which swept down from her head on either side to form twin eaves, which thrust out like the wings of some ebony pagoda; and in her hair were also small gold pieces. She came bearing rice and fruit and leavened bread which we might eat with our own food, her gown loosely drapped about her and exposing half her bosom; and twice she glanced sidelong at me with a question in her eyes. White men are rich, and give their money freely.

When eating was done the Malinke men played music, squatting in the courtyard just outside the door where the concubines and relatives had gathered; and Seaku talked of the ancient glories of nearby Djenne, once a famous entrepôt of gold and slaves and merchandise, founded by the Dias; of dervishes and dancing girls, and how black troops from Senegal broke a white man's strike in France, cracking heads with rifle-butts and filleting the pockets of the fallen.

"I have been a traveller," he said, "but it is better to live in a peaceful place, with friends, than travel among the mischief of the world."

"But are you happy here?"

"Happy? A strange question, Monsieur Blanc." He stared out into the courtyard for some seconds. "Happy, a little, yes; but I was happier in Senegal, in my own village."

"But you prosper here?"

"Oh, I prosper here. I am the leading baker of the town, I have cattle and this house, and three concubines, I am respected. Respected, monsieur, not loved. My cattle do not love me, nor my concubines, although I feed them well; and here I am a stranger, these are not my people. I love the people of my village far away in Senegal, and they love me too, so happiness is there, not here. My heart is there."

"Then happiness springs from love?"

He pondered his reply. "Monsieur, if I make bread without salt, it is poor bread and I throw it away. If a man lives without hope, his life is poor and he throws it away. Hope is the salt of life. But as yeast will make bread rise, so will love make a man rise; with love he can rise above himself, above selfishness, his heart swells and becomes big, and he finds happiness. Only a man who loves well, and is well loved, monsieur, can find happiness … and no man can be happy if his heart lies in another place, apart from him."

Unhappy, then, is the man whose heart lies on the far horizon, and always moves ahead.

The Malinke men slept somewhere else, I slept in the room alone; and twice she came, once with water and again with tea; she tickled my toes with a straw while I drank the tea, and lingered for a time, then went away.

To love, and be loved … how much did the baker know?

"Where to?" I asked the captain, a beardless Songhai lad from far down-river.

"To Gao, God willing," he replied. "We sail at noon; will you come?"

Gao? Clearly one must go to Gao, since the river and the road both went that way; and Gao was the gate to paradise, and if not paradise, then Europe. I paid the fare, a bagatelle, bought chickens and rice and a blanket, and joined the passengers and crew to help with the final loading of the cargo.

For seven leisurely days we travelled with the river, slipping through sandy shallows past small islands, murmuring down green lanes amid the barren solitude; fifteen passengers and the captain perched on top of bags of rice and wheat, and the captain's boy sat at the tiller; we slept at night by small and poorly villages or in the wilderness, by fires. The days were an idle pageant of new and pleasant places, the river and the stars were our companions through the nights.

Dusk might bring us to some nameless place, a group of huts, a nomad camp; the passengers would go ashore and say their prayers, and share a fire to cook their evening meal. The people of the place would come, with murmured greetings, and stand politely in the shadows before squatting nearer to the fire, absorbing the conversation of far places and offering the wisdom of old men. When all had eaten and the fire was low, and another boat had slipped in for the night, the villagers would drift away and one by one we rolled up in our blankets and slept on the sandy ground.

At dawn pale tongues of river-mist licked gently at the waters. Early fishermen with nets and snares entered their canoes and paddled out among the mists. The sleeping figures stirred, and presently arose and washed, and spread their tiny prayer-mats, facing the rising sun, to say their prayers. The housewife in the covered *pirogue* which came in late last night crawls out from the boat's reed canopy, yawns, scoops up water to splash her face, and kneels to pray; she is pregnant, and does not have to stand. Her husband comes out too, and with an angry scowl points out what any fool can see: she is facing south-west, instead of east. Women come, wrapped in sombre robes against the chill of early dawn, wearing rags and ornaments of gold and bearing gourds of milk in which small balls of butter float. Hair and dust float in the milk, and often enough there is cow-dung in the bottom of the gourd, but this is not a matter for dispute. With much winding and coughing and farting the motor is coaxed to life, and we fare out on the river once again.

Beyond a great marsh of reeds where horses and herds of cattle grazed, where the sky was darkened, by swarms of birds and fish popped from the river as if they could not all fit in the water at one time, we came upon the horizonless expanse of Lake Debo. The river entered the lake where a pinnacle of rock thrust up from the waste of reeds, the island of Tone-oli, snagged with boulders and scabbed with rough mat huts round the base and on high places, and tenanted by black people clad in rags and nesting, like birds, amid their filth.

"They are pirates," said the captain, frowning nervously towards them. "They live by stealing cattle, and raid passing river traffic." He smiled, a little proudly. "But we have a motor, so they will have no thoughts of us."

But some miles farther on the motor died. The water was too deep to pole and we had no paddles, and there was no one amongst us who understood machines. The boat drifted slowly, and scraped on to a sandy bar beside an island. Prayers were said, the sun went down, and the captain's boy came up to me and said, "Patron, have you eaten the captain?"

What villainy was this?

"No, he is there." I pointed to the captain who was hanging a magic charm on the dead motor. The boy was puzzled.

"How can one eat the captain?" I demanded "He is not dead. Shall we kill him?"

The boy burst out laughing; *le capitaine*, it seemed, was a species of large fish, and men had waded ashore to cook some on the island. So we ate the captain, after all, and prepared to spend the night aboard the boat; that we were stranded on a sandbar was a matter of no moment, but merely the will of Allah and therefore logical. We might drift off during the night and wake up on another, but it would be the same thing; out here under the stars, with a full belly and chewing kola-nut, nothing really mattered. Storks were nesting on the island, and swift flights of ibis, duck, and pelican, abdim storks and spoonbills were winging overhead towards the sunset.

Other evenings had exhausted talk of trade and horses, and how a donkey may be mated with a mare, and this night it turned to women.

"I have been to Marrakesh in Morocco," said a bearded trader, "and have seen a thousand women in three or four small streets called the Busbiah, fighting among themselves for the love of men who visit them. For three hundred francs, or less, one may have the favours of any one of a thousand girls: yellow girls, white, black, girls from any country in the world, even from places whose names are too distant to remember.

"In Dakar," another volunteered, "I have seen black girls, and some half white, who are bought as slaves in Portuguese Guinea and Spanish Mauretania, and taken as dancing-girls to the pleasure-houses of Dakar."

The boy wriggled on his perch of bags.

"I have been to Kumasi, on the British side, and one can find women there for a hundred francs, or even fifty."

Someone muttered disbelievingly.

"There is an island in the sea," I said, "called Corisco, the Island of Love, south and east of here. On this island there are virgins crying out for men, and a man may have a girl there in the name of pleasure only."

This sally was greeted with cynical amusement, for virgins rarely gave themselves for pleasure; and a cattle-trader said, "There is a village far north in the desert, an oasis called Mutah; and here the women are so strong, and fond of strangers, that they will pay for a traveller to share their bed."

A gale of laughter swept the boat and startled nearby birds: here, then, was the original Prince of Liars. Another said, more soberly, "The Susu women in the south are the most beautiful I know."

"The Daga women of Timbuktu are the most beautiful in the Sudan, and therefore the world," declared another. "They are as queens, and jinn, who tempt a man and spoil him for all others."

Timbuktu?

"Where is Timbuktu?" I asked. "Is it far from here?"

"We pass near by," the captain said. "Three more days down-river, and five hours- march inland."

Ah, Timbuktu: I had thought it would be far away, far north where none but caravans could go; but already we were far north, and soon we would be farther. Allah willing. Timbuktu, the Queen of Sudan, the Light of the Niger Valley, the final goal of the longest road a traveller might take …

"I will go to Timbuktu, then, not Gao."

∧∧∧∧∧∧∧

"You have been here in Timbuktu for some time," said the Commandant, "yet you failed to report. All visitors must report, and usually do; it is not pleasant for me to have to summon them." He was a moon-faced officer of middle age and agreeable formality; but his manner, although friendly, was severe. "Have you been staying at the guesthouse?"

The guesthouse was an empty bungalow in an adobe compound, run by two swarthy individuals from Martinique; but though I had paid for a room I had not slept in it.

"I have a room there."

"But you prefer to camp outside. Is that it?"

"The room is occupied by animals."

He looked up. "Animals, monsieur?"

"Mice, and lice, and lizards," I said bluntly, and with truth.

"Indeed. So you sleep in the gardens by the mosque?"

"No one seems to mind."

"And how long do you intend to stay in Timbuktu, sleeping in a garden, eating in the market-place, and walking through the streets with melons on your head?"

I had been observed, then, amid delighted laughter, balancing great melons on my head: an admirable feat requiring diligence and skill.

"Monsieur," the Commandant continued, "there is in Timbuktu, especially in Timbuktu, a certain matter of prestige which we Frenchmen must uphold; there are only forty of us here; and certain standards of common sense and dignity are required of Europeans who come here." He endorsed my passport, and held it out to me.

"I invite you to leave the town as soon as possible. I invite you, quite strongly, to spend this night in the guesthouse, and to assume a responsible attitude until you leave us. Thank you."

The moon was down, the night was still, the stars were chips of electric blue like shattered beryls drowning in old purple; the desert dunes were bare and smooth, the city was washed in gentle light and draped with indigo. The streets were empty, the market was bare; well-wrapped cocoons of homeless men snored in sandy places, and drowsy camels rumbled damply as one passed, but the city was asleep and only ghosts and sentries were abroad.

The desert was the acolyte of Time, and therefore ageless, but wrinkled shadows lined the city's furrowed walls as if the years were on parade, and the centuries found refuge in the scattered shards of palaces and tombs. Men had sought for knowledge here, and combed each other's brains with deft inquiry; but had they found the thing which all were seeking? Knowledge is as a spot of light, and increasing knowledge will cause the light to grow, its contact with the darkness ever greater; but as the light grows stronger yet, and stronger, so the shadows cast are deeper still, and longer: and is the thing which all men seek a mere illusion, a phantom which eludes inspection as a shadow shrinks from light?

Happiness belongs to paradise, said Mohmoud; and Kader thought it was some magic herb, the baker said it was the child of love; aye, one might taste it briefly in the Grape, but only briefly, and with sorrow as its foil. Some thought its natural habitat was in the soul of man; others, that it was a mere condition of the mind: but where was Soul, and what was Mind?

A sentry challenged me, moving slowly from the shadows, and I walked beyond the fort towards the gardens by the mosque.

The night was warm, but the garden hollow held a pocket of cool air fragrant with the mingled smell of flowers. The henna shrubs spilt honey on the shadows, the cloying scent of oleanders was as incense haunting tall black temple columns, and the perfumes of basil and mint and mustard-plant ebbed and flowed on unseen tides. I lay in a shadowed place where orange-trees dripped blossoms on the sand, gazing up at the fronds of palms and the glittering stars which crowded close above. The silence of the gardens betrayed the cautious movement of small creatures and absorbed the sleepy orchestration of the frogs; somewhere in town a girl cried out in terror, then cried out no more, and a distant jackal howled. Starlight flecked the foliage with silver, touching a pomegranate-tree with magic and turning the fruit to goblets of dark wine.

It was good to lie there in the sand, companion to the night in her boudoir; in the Garden of Birds there dwelt elusive happiness, and the taste had been rich and sweet; but happiness would come no more, I knew. The Commandant would see to that. Something was at an end, a symphony was finished: in the morning I would leave, at dawn, companion to the sun. By boat, perhaps, by caravan if there was one, or on foot ... to the north. Why, Anna had gone north: and the way there would be paved with the wealth of spring.

Green, green things ... the gift of Allah, a silence in the soul ... the frogs seemed drowsy, distant now, throbbing like muted drums, calling, far away along the road to Anywhere.

THE LAWLESS AND THE LOTUS

POOLING THE PUBLISHING FEES from his three travel books, Peter Pinney bought a schooner in Central America and spent 1957 and 1958 running contraband whiskey and cigarettes from the Panama Canal Zone into neighbouring Costa Rica and Colombia. These adventures became the basis of his novel *Ride the Volcano*. In 1961 he commenced his homeward romp, detailed in *The Lawless and the Lotus*. Travelling via St Kitts and various islands of the British and French West Indies, he was expelled from the Caribbean, and ended up in Tahiti. The final, audacious leg of his journey, as a stowaway through the islands of the French Pacific, is the crowning escapade of his fifteen year "rogue's progress".

NEVIS ISLAND

"Where you travelled?" Wiseman's sardonic tone was undisguisedly discourteous.

"Here and there."

"Europe? Asia?"

"Yes."

He grunted disapprovingly. "Africa? You been to Lagos? Algiers? Mozambique?"

I nodded, familiar with the form of inquisition and its aim. He would be one of those who travelled in order to have travelled, a name-dropper whose persistent social trick was to litanise the names of distant places he had — or had not — seen. His suitcase, if he had one, would be swarming with a salad of bright labels.

"Bangkok? 'Frisco? Sydney?"

"Sydney?" Sydney, Nova Scotia, I had never seen. Sydney, Australia, was my home.

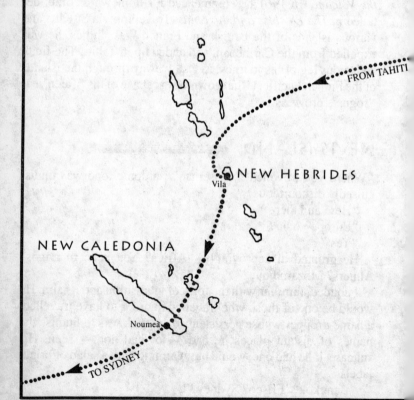

PACIFIC   OCEAN

FROM TAHITI

NEW HEBRIDES
Vila

NEW CALEDONIA

Noumea

TO SYDNEY

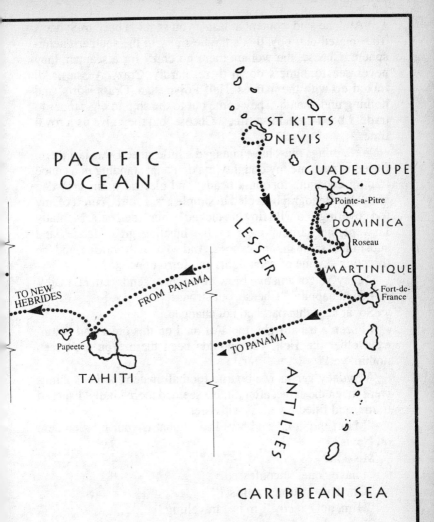

PACIFIC
OCEAN

ST KITTS
NEVIS

GUADELOUPE
Pointe-a-Pitre

LESSER

DOMINICA
Roseau

MARTINIQUE
Fort-de-France

TO NEW
HEBRIDES   FROM PANAMA

Papeete

TO PANAMA

TAHITI

ANTILLES

CARIBBEAN SEA

NOT TO SCALE

"Ah," he said, content at last, "you shoulda been to Sydney. You missed out, boy, that's the best city in the southern hemisphere. Cheese, the women there go crazy for a seaman, they never see foreigners down there, hardly. Crazy Aussies. All mixed up with the natives. Half Polynesian. Grass skirts, and nothing underneath. They come out to the ship in big canoes to trade. I been there lotsa times. Cheese, but they give us a royal time."

Well, things must have changed a little since I was last there. I tried to imagine my doughty maiden aunt standing in a canoe trading coconuts for glass beads; and electric trains crowded with chic stenographers clad in simple grass skirts, bereft of any top covering and with flowers tucked behind their ears. Mentally I swept the harbour clear of the bustling green ferries and substituted sampans and canoes. And what of the bridge, and the thrusting skyline of neon lights and ferro-concrete?

"They've got a native brew down there sends 'em all mad," he added happily. "Cheese, but strong!"

So, at least that part had not changed.

"I seen a tribal fight, too. All mad on this brew and beltin' each other up. Hell, you shoulda been there. You ain't seen nothin' yet!"

A Sydney versus Melbourne football match: perhaps things were much the same, after all. He seemed more kindly disposed to me, and filled my glass with beer.

"May I inquire," said Mrs Pea, "what is your mission here on Nevis?"

Mission?

"I have none," I confessed.

"Oh. Then you're a tourist?"

"H'm, not exactly. I'm just travelling."

She eyed me with the beginnings of suspicion.

"But, I mean, you're not just a beachcomber, of course. Or a vagabond, or anything like that."

She looked at me expectantly, but I sipped my beer in silence. I had no great taste for such egregious inquisition; let her feed upon her own imagination.

"I keep a respectable house," she said finally, ruffling her feathers, "and I like to know a little of my guests." She broke

off, suddenly suspicious, and plucked vigorously at her neck
while an expression of concern crossed her face. "But ... your
name is Pinney too?"

"Yes."

"Could ... I mean, were they any relation to you, the Pinneys
who lived here?"

"Yes, same family." Or at least a close branch of it. "I thought
I might visit the old estate while I'm here."

It had been the second largest estate on the island, and
included four miles of beach known then and now as Pinney's
Beach, but when the island was devastated by volcanic gas the
family fled to North America.

"But I didn't know." She breathed, eyes wide with crisis.
"My God, I never thought —"

"Of course."

"Oh, my dear gentleman, you must forgive me I never suspected for a moment."

"Oh, but I'll make you so welcome!" she cried, regaining her
composure. "You'll have the finest room, the best my house can
offer. Oh yes, we'll arrange a party too." Anticipation cleansed
her face with joy. "You'll be able to meet all the best people.
Everyone will come. And where is your family now? Where did
they go from Nevis?"

"North America, and then Australia. My home is in Sydney,
Australia."

Wiseman chirruped like a plundered squirrel.

"Sydney?"

"Aye. We wear grass skirts and paddle canoes, you might
remember. Perhaps you saw me there."

"Uh ... yeah, well ..."

"Excuse me," I said standing up.

"Of course." Perhaps they thought I wished to use the toilet,
but I walked right out of the door and into the street, leaving them
with the privilege of paying for three beers; and, though one
came to the door and called after me, I walked on without caring
to look back.

∿∿∿∿∿

The island is an old volcano thrusting upwards from the sea, and Columbus named it Nieves for the white clouds which, formed by condensation of moist air rising up its flanks, stream out like snowy pennants from its peak. The dark greens of the upper slopes melt into softer pastel lowlands patched with sugar-cane and cotton, and fringed with cocos palms.

At little more than a mile was the entrance of the estate, and a roughly contrived notice said, "Entry Forbidden. Except for Buying Shells, or on Special business." The way led in through groves of coconut and bananas and clammy-cherry-trees to a scraggle of shacks set amid the stone ruins and tamarind-trees of what had once been a great estate. John Wade, the current owner, was a stalwart young Negro who lived in one of the shacks with his wife and a chuckle of small infants. I told him who I was, and why I came: at first he was ill at ease, doubtless wondering if I hoped to claim the place, but soon regained his confidence and proudly told me what he knew. The first Pinney to come here had originally been imprisoned as a rebel and banished after Monmouth's defeat at Sedgemoor, but secured these lands and prospered with coffee, sugar-cane, and copra. He and his descendants held the land for a hundred and sixty years, but history's only comments were chiselled on a scattering of graves.

"Once ago it was a big, big place," said John. "It had a sugar-mill, and hundred acres' coconuts, and arl. Two Englishmen called Bone and Walwyn had it once, and then two Syrian rascals called Carvarjo, and then my father bought it. Mostly we makes copra — pointing to crude drying sheds — and sells the shells for fuel. We used to lease some land for people to grow sugar-cane, and cotton, but they never pay no rent, so now we put cattle there to graze."

"No old books or anything left, I suppose? No records?"

"No records. We done forget those people now."

As well, perhaps. The lot of the Negro slave had not been pretty. I put my hand on his shoulder and he grinned with embarrassment, and the thought came to me that here was the scion of Negro slaves in proud command of property once owned by whites who whipped his forebears; and here was the son of those distant whites, a landless stranger come to visit the grey ruins. What price the fleeting arrogance of those who held the lash? The conquerors were conquered, the Negroes had endured. He had paraphrased the history of my clan, We done forget those people now.

"Up there," he said, pointing farther up the slopes, "is the ruins of the big house."

The big house "once ago" must have been quite a formidable mansion, a two-storeyed building of cut stone looking down on Charlestown and the verdant coastal belt dark against the Caribbean Sea. Starlings nested in the creviced walls and plants grew in damp crannies, the interior was thick with seeds and brush. Attending the large building were quarters where slaves had slept; there was a curious hexagonal kitchen, with underneath a grim little dungeon where unruly slaves were chained.

Had they been happy here, those English exiles? They had prospered in this alien place, with their slaves and cane. Here they had wed and banqueted and died. But in the isolation of this once splendid house, bearing the white man's burden on the backs of Negro slaves and overshadowed by the mighty volcano, had they known peace?

The place was consumed by silence, no ghosts appeared, the stones which knew the answers would not speak.

We done forget those people now.

/\/\/\/\/\/\

SCHOONER YVONNE MARIE

Alltok scowled at me from under lowered brows. He was less dark than the other crewmen, rangy and lean, a man of prolonged silences broken by explosive bursts of passion.

"What you t'inkin' about, white marn?"

It was at once a query and a challenge. Conrad moved uneasily, watching us.

"I was wondering," I said carefully, "if Thomas the cook has a big, big pot."

"Big pot? What for you wanna big pot?"

"Because I think maybe we're going to have to carve you up and eat you. And you look too damn' tough to eat raw."

His eyes bulged.

"Eat me?" Dramatically he laid one bony hand across his heart, leaning forward on his haunches to stare in utter surprise. "Me?"

I stifled a grin, saying, "Because, if we keep on our present course, we're going to be at sea a long time. So I figure we'll run out of food. We can eat the captain first, because he's fat; and then we'll eat you."

Slowly, quite slowly, a grin of understanding spread throughout his face, and he sat back on his heels and laughed.

"Ho, bloody white marn carnibal, gonna eat a black marn! Ho-ho, eat a captain fus', because he fat." He stabbed a finger at Conrad. "You fus' inna pot, captain. Ha-ha!"

Had I offered him mere courtesy, he would probably have scorned me. But he had a sense of humour, and the risk had been worth while.

"Too tough!" he chuckled happily. "Yeah, marn, I pretty tough. More better eat the captain fus', he sof' and fat. Hey, white marn, you like more coffee?"

MARTINIQUE

From one corner of the Savanne a headland of immense black rock thrusts strongly south into the sea. The cliffs are surmounted by the walls and battlements of a formidable old fortress, fabled Fort St Louis. Beyond a thicket of trees and tucked away behind a corner, I found a gloomy entrance in the stonework. A notice stated, "Entry fifty francs".

One shilling. But what was there inside?

"What is this place?" I asked an elderly gentleman near by, and he smiled kindly.

"But it is the museum, it is a place of great history. There you will find the history of La Martinique."

Two rough mulatto scoundrels passed us bearing a basket of raw meat between them, offal and bones which gave forth a sour smell and dripped darkly on the gravel.

"There are some animals too," he explained. "But they are

not of great interest. The museum is unique, and well worth fifty francs."

I thanked him and followed the two men through the arched stone entrance. In a tall and cavernous antechamber there was a ticket-seller's booth, but no one yet in attendance, so I turned and made my way up the shallow stone stairs of a gently sloping tunnel.

An iron-barred gate led to a sunlit eminence above, and here, at peace from prodding crowds and washed by the sea breeze, were the animals and birds and reptiles of Martinique's two-year-old zoo.

There were cages holding birds and I paused by one; inside was a diver, black and white, but a sorry specimen. His plumage was in disarray, one eye was sightless, and the rough concrete had worn his webbed feet away to stumps, so that he only moved when aroused, and immediately sat down. Poor diver then: instead of the wide ocean, he had only a quarter inch of slime in a shallow trough, but at least he had protection from his natural enemies.

Next door was a malfini, a goshawk, sleeping in the sun. I had swum in the sea below the Fort, and the sun was warm on my back. But did the goshawk have no water? His dish was dry. Well, they would give him water during the morning rounds.

There was an egret. One leg appeared to be broken, and its frail body was racked with recurring spasms. It tottered back and forth on one leg, thrusting at shadows with its beak, attacking unseen enemies: if ever a bird was mad, it was mad. Could isolation from its kind affect a creature thus? Could birds be afflicted with neuroses such as plagued us humans?

Two deer were in a small, fenced enclosure, dainty creatures which nuzzled among the straw and ate the fragrant mauve blossoms which fell from a cedar-tree above. There were two manicou, or possums, in a cage and both were sick, but one of them lay in its dry water trough in deathly lassitude, heedless of drying scraps of meat near by. It was almost hairless, and a great ulcer at its brow presented it from closing its right eye. I found the half of a banana and tossed it near the creature's head. Perhaps a minute passed. Then in horrible, slow pantomime it tried to rise, moving its hideous, hairless head to and fro, blindly bumped the banana several times with its nose, and as slowly opened its mouth and commenced to weakly mumble the food. It experienced much difficulty in pulping and swallowing even a peeled portion of a ripe banana; its entire machinery had slowed, run down, until scarcely a spark of life remained.

A shiver of revulsion trickled down my spine and I moved on to the next cage, and the next. What kind of place was this? The baboon had only his urine to drink, the wildcat next door had nothing at all, their cages were foul with the stench of accumulated dung, and their fur matted with the squashed faeces on which they walked and lay. Did no one clean these cages? Was water never provided, did they merely live on rain? Something was terribly wrong. Grimly I stalked here and there to confirm my worst suspicions. This zoo was nothing more nor less than a concentration camp of hapless creatures, enduring varying degrees of hunger, thirst, sickness, filth, and misery.

Birds of diverse nature were caged together, so confined that the weaker could not escape the strong; a constant social torture reduced the weaker to shivering, jerking neurotics. Pecking, feather-pulling, blinding one another: birds could be quite human, I discovered. For hours on end one seabird offered a single straw to his crazed mate. The hope, the pathetic dead hope! Always the slime to drink, or nothing. Some monkeys were crammed in tiny, stinking cages with nothing to eat or drink; they mewed piteously as I passed, and thrust out tiny, clutching hands.

Saurians and reptiles existed in a form of catatonic suspension: the birds and animals were the ones to suffer. Until, like humans, suffering became unendurable, and they went out of their minds. Many animals had no water, a few carnivores had nothing but rotting, unwanted bread or bananas to eat. Apparently the attendants feared many of the beasts, and those cages were never cleaned; the inmates lived in an evil-smelling swamp of their own filth, often with nothing to eat but rotting garbage, and their only drink was slime befouled with urine.

How could they have survived for two long years in these conditions? How many had died? How many were dying now?

The white rats, the pacas, and those monkeys in larger cages seemed well fed, special pets perhaps, with plenty of stale bread and water too. But the two racoons: two hapless sentries endlessly pacing opposite ends of their cage ankle-deep in filth: their water trough held nothing but a dried dark-green scum ... Shall one have pity for a jackal? The ceaseless hunt up and down, three paces one way and three paces back from dawn to dusk; he drank when it happened to rain. Some bird of exotic plumage was so weak, it fell with its head twisted underneath its body, quivering.

I approached one of the attendants, stretched out asleep on a bench; the basket of offal was gathering flies in the sun. I nudged him roughly, an he sat up.

"When do you feed them?" I demanded.

"Uh?" He looked around sleepily, and stared at me. "You done buy ticket?"

"I'll buy one. When do you feed the animals?"

"Soon, maybe. When people come. Saturday, maybe visitors come, then I give food. You want buy soft drink? Ice-cream? I got for sale."

So the week-ends, when the visitors came, were the big days for the zoo's unfortunates. They were fed then.

"When do you give them water? I want to know. You'd better tell me."

Sweet blue eyes, must there be another fight?

"Rain every day," he said in disinterest, and lay back again on the bench. "What I care for damn' animals? If you no want to buy something, I got no interest for talk."

A squall of temper sizzled through me. No care for animals? Why, this piece of idle filth was only concerned with selling refreshments to visitors: he had no concern for suffering creatures. They could slowly die of thirst and misery and disease, and he would pay no heed. Deliberately I put my hands in my pockets and kept them there.

Turning on my heel, I walked away, down the stone tunnel and out of the Fort. In a nearby market I purchased a sackful of fruit, returned, apportioned it among the herbivores, and commenced filling the drinking troughs with a hose which I discovered by a tap. The churl came and tried to snatch the hose from my hand.

"*Meutre alors*!" he cried angrily. "I don't need no help. What you think you doing, you own this place? Hey?"

He wrenched at the hose, and I resisted, so then he went to

turn off the tap. I watched him quietly as the hose fell slack, the flow of water ceased. He stood waiting to see what I would do.

The familiar repetition of a pattern: the strength of my own convictions hurled bodily against those of another man. What form of selfish conceit possessed me, that I sought to take the affairs of the zoo in my own hands? For two whole years it had survived without me: why must my arrival precipitate a crisis?

Setting down the hose, I walked towards him, and he darted glances about as if seeking for a weapon. Drawing close to him, I halted, took my wallet forth, and offered him a note for one hundred francs.

"If you would be so good," I asked politely, "as to permit my little madness, and accept this small gift for the loan of the hose, I would be grateful."

He eyed me warily, gingerly reached for the note and his dark face creased with an engaging smile.

"But of course, monsieur," he said with satisfaction, pocketing the bill. "Any time, monsieur, any time."

When the water troughs were full and the cages hosed to a cleaner state, I went away. It was not, after all, my affair. What possible concern could an Australian have with a zoo on Martinique? Here I was a guest in this pleasant city. What possible excuse could I have for interfering in the affairs of others? The zoo was the private affair of the people who lived on this island: I was an intruder, it had nothing to do with me.

∧∧∧∧∧∧∧

As dusk grew nigh, I entered the Fort and concealed myself in a tiny room, adjoining the long stone tunnel. No one had seen me, no one could know I was there; the girl who sold tickets had gone home, the two attendants were up in the zoo. The time was five minutes to seven. At seven o'clock the Fort's huge doors would be closed and locked for the night.

During the afternoon I had wandered through the zoo, to discover that conditions were possibly even worse than they were two weeks ago. The malfini was dead, the diver lay on its side with glazed eyes, two of the monkeys were close to death and surely the wretched manicou could not last the night. Few of the creatures had any water, none of the cages had been cleaned. I distributed fruit and water, paying another hundred francs, then made a careful reconnaissance which assured me the attendants slept elsewhere, and withdrew. Now I had slipped back inside the Fort intent on committing a crime.

The three-minute warning-bell rang, and half a dozen visitors shuffled down the tunnel. I crouched low behind an empty showcase, but if anyone entered the tiny room I must be seen. Minutes passed. Somewhere an iron gate clanged, and the two attendants walked briskly down the tunnel.

What excitement there would be, if they found me crouching there.

There was the click of a master switch somewhere near at hand, and all the lights were doused. They made their way down to the antechamber, footsteps echoing through the dark stone vault: the main doors slammed with a clatter, and a key rattled in the lock.

I was inside the Fort alone, and the entire night was at my disposal. I could fire this social haystack at my leisure, then doubtless devise some means of escaping over the walls.

Blood of a ghoul, but it was dark!

Night had fixed itself batlike on the Fort, and the tunnel was of unrelieved blackness. Gingerly I groped my way from the little room and moved up the steps with quickened pulse, through a cloistered series of chambers and on to the upper exit which gave onto the zoo.

I entered the zoo enclosure, perhaps fifty yards by eighty, and went towards the cages which held birds. Most of the cage doors were held by simple latches, some swinging out on common hinges and others sliding up like traps; and now I set myself to releasing all those creatures who conditions were the worst. But not the carnivores, or animals which might endanger children who came to play in the Savanne close by the Fort.

The seagulls first. They were sleepy and suspicious, and refused to leave their cages until I disturbed them with a stick. Terns and gulls and others limped and fluttered from open doors and blundered off in the night: there was the joy of a strong conviction in my heart as I watched them go. An owl was next, and he went quickly; the egret with the broken leg seemed unable to move. Many other birds I freed, but left all those which were healthier than the rest.

The deer were nervous as I moved about, and three ducks chittered softly in alarm. Beyond the deer's enclosure was a low stone parapet and a brace of ancient cannon, and from here one could look down on a sports arena where girls were playing basketball in the light of powerful arc-lamps. This way, I suspected, would provide me with escape.

Two large boa constrictors were examining their cage inch by inch, rats scampered about the grounds searching for scraps of food. I opened the door of the skunk's cage. He could not escape the zoo, but there were many places to hide, and I grinned as I envisioned the protest he might make at being captured. The foxes, no, I would leave them, they would slaughter the weaker ones. The two racoons were freed; bewildered for a minute, they finally scurried off at desperate speed. Two pacas were loosed, and hurtled around the compound with the three-legged dog lolloping uncertainly in pursuit.

Ha, there would be panic in the morning!

Steps led down to a sunken pit where carnivores and a crocodile were kept, and other beasts. The wildcat and the large baboon I did not dare release, but there were miserable monkeys dying of neglect, and these were given freedom. Some could scarcely be coaxed from their filthy dens, so weak and diseased they were, but others began to move about and consider the walls and trees. The spider monkeys I left alone, they had a large cage and seemed to be keepers' pets. The surviving possum I chased from its sty, and it furtively stole away and disappeared. Other creatures I might have chosen were secured behind stout locks, and neither of the keys I had would fit.

A certain amount of subdued excitement was growing throughout the zoo. There were rustlings in the trees and a scampering through grass, and furry bodies darted to and fro in a dither of agitation. A heinous act? I laughed delightedly and wished them well.

The floodlights had been doused, the wall below the parapet was dark. It led down to a ledge thick with shrubs and trees. I found some long rods of soft iron, twisted one around the muzzle of a cannon, and by securing a second rod to the first made myself an iron rope which led over the parapet to the ledge below.

I eased over the parapet like some mediaeval villain escaping prison walls, and carefully slid down to the ledge below. Dripping with perspiration, I sat a while to rest, and comb my hair; then chose a moment when the headlights of a car had just passed by to scale the gates at the foot of the step, drop lightly to the street and walk away in darkness.

By the gods, what a strange way to spend an evening on Martinique!

In the morning the campaign was carried into the heart of the enemy's camp. In the office of Chez Chêneaux Reynal I announced, "I look for a Monsieur Roget Petit-Jean. I understand he is President of the Historical and Geographical Society."

The society was in command of the museum and the zoo. Monsieur Petit-Jean, a bland-faced gentleman of about fifty, sufficiently polite, listened with composure to my questions. Yes, he was the President, and the society was responsible for the zoo. Would I not sit down?

"Have you been there lately?" I inquired.

He was puzzled. "Well, no. No. I am occupied with pressing affairs, you understand."

"Then permit me to inform you that the condition of the animals there is absolutely criminal," I said severely. Aye, I would stand up and be counted. "Animals and birds there are dying of neglect. Are you aware of this?"

He was agreeably polite. "But no. You see, I have no direct —"

"And yet you are supposed to be in charge? Then permit me to inform you further. Last night I entered the zoo and released a number of birds and animals. Let them loose from their cages. You comprehend?"

He regarded me with mild astonishment. "You released them?"

"Yes. And furthermore, if conditions do not rapidly improve, I shall go there again and let the rest go, including the carnivores."

But he evidenced no spasm of excitement. He gazed at me inquiringly, as if wondering what advantage I might hope to gain by this invasion, and protested calmly:

"But … it is not my affair, monsieur. Yes, I am President, but I am not the supervisor of the zoo. I have no direct dealings with it. And I am quite sure … the supervisor is an admirable man. I am sure —"

"Who is the supervisor?"

"Père Pinchon, of the Seminary College. He is a qualified naturalist, a most admirable man."

"Then I shall go to him. And, remember, you've been given fair warning."

Outside, I hailed a taxi and was carried off towards the college on heights above the city. Merely releasing a few birds and animals was not enough; taken by itself, it was only an act of mischief, which would certainly not produce lasting good. Discovery of the outrage would be muffled by the thick walls of the Fort, the crime would be buried in silence away from the gaze of men, no one would ever see it as a form of angry protest. Attention must be drawn to the zoo's miserable state, or my action would be no more than indulgence in irresponsible folly.

Alors, I would beard this Père Pinchon.

On the third floor of one wing of the college the priest was engaged in lecturing a classroom full of boys; I waited a few minutes while he finished. As I stood on the balcony, I could see him through a window, a stout young man with a fine spade beard, a rich full-throated voice and twinkling eyes, attired in khaki shirt and shorts. He seemed vigorous and intelligent and glad of his role as tutor: why then had he let the zoo become such a wretched shambles?

I greeted him as he came out from the classroom, and he beamed with instant courtesy and came to grasp my hand. The zoo? He observed me warily. Yes he agreed, he was in charge; and his smile faded, his eyes narrowed in a level, flinty stare.

"Conditions there are a disgrace to everything you stand for," I stated flatly. "It is a scene of criminal negligence. I came to ask you why."

"Why is what?" he boomed, and glared at me from head to toe. "What right do you have to make this accusation?"

"By the right of any man to protest the torture of animals. The cages are swamps of excreta, the two cretins you employ as keepers never fill the water troughs, and when they think to pass around food they don't even know which animals eat meat and which are herbivores."

"Nonsense!" he exploded. "*Mon Dieu*, but it is *formidable*, Nonsense, I say!" He gazed at me indignantly. "Who are you? What gives you the right to come here with ... this ..."

"I'm no one of importance," I snapped. "Just a flea in your ear; but I'm out for blood. I'm not here to entertain you with mistruths. I've made a detailed inspection of your zoo. It's incredible! It's inexcusable! Most animals have had no water at all for two whole weeks, except rain," I pointed out, wondering if this was actually true. "They only survive, because it rains. The fox doesn't even have a water dish, and the racoons' dish is broken. What of that?"

He hesitated. Doubt appeared in his attitude.

"Well," he hedged, "sometimes there is no water. The zoo is at a height, the water mains are faulty, they are sometimes under repair."

Ah, so I had him there! I stared at him cynically until he looked away. Father Pinchon, a dominating figure to a classroom of small boys, did not care to be challenged in this fashion. Good.

"That compound is a private little hell of misery, filth, and torment. Why do you starve the animals? Why are they given no medical attention? You're a naturalist, you look fairly intelligent, why do you let them die?"

"What animals?" he demanded with renewed vigour. "Come now, be specific. What animals?"

"The malifini; it died of neglect. The diver, it died of neglect. The egret with the broken leg. A manicou that had an ulcerated eye has died. Two rhesus monkeys are almost dead. Shall I go on?"

He stared out over the balcony at boys playing in the yard below, and doubtless he wished that he was with them.

"How can we manage everything," he said finally, "on the few funds we have? I have not the time, I must teach my classes, and there is not enough money. There are many things besides the zoo. We have to struggle along with what we have, as best we can."

He was fat enough; he looked as if he struggled very well.

"Then if you can't find the time, and you can't afford a zoo," I said bitterly, "get rid of it. Give the creatures away, destroy them cleanly, anything. You have no right to take God's creatures and condemn them to slow death by starvation, thirst and disease, just because you don't have the time or the money to give them proper care. There's a quarter of a million people on this island. If each contributed five francs every year, you'd have enough to make that zoo a decent, well-run place. And if the people of Martinique aren't sufficiently interested to contribute a penny a year, they're obviously not interested in having a zoo at all."

"Oh, but they are interested. Many people visit the zoo."

"At fifty francs a visit. What happens to the money?"

He fidgeted uncomfortably. There was a long moment of silence.

"And here's something else," I said, "If you don't improve conditions in your zoo, I'm going to liberate all the birds and animals. Every last one of them. You comprehend?"

At once he snapped to attention. He fixed me with a piercing gaze and jabbed his finger at my chest.

"You are the imbecile!" he cried excitedly. "Eh? You were the one? You released the animals and birds last night?"

"But, of course, who else?"

He was dumbfounded. This kind of nonsense appeared to be beyond his experience. He opened his mouth several times before he found words to put in it.

"But this is a matter for the police!" he burst forth.

"Of course."

"I will have to inform the police, you understand. I have no other recourse, I am obliged to report you."

"*D'accord*, let's both go at once to the police. You can tell them about my crime, and I'll tell them about yours."

He led the way along the balcony, but paused with a worried frown.

"It is very serious," he insisted, glancing at me strangely.

"It is," I agreed. "That is why I am here."

He went a little farther and stopped again, asking for my name.

"My name is unimportant, and so am I, and so are you. Only our crimes are important."

"But I must give your name to the police," he declared, pausing afresh at the head of a flight of steps.

"I will do that for you. And you can tell them yours."

For a moment he seemed lost in thought, frowning down at the steps, then abruptly turned and disappeared inside a room near by. I waited about a minute, then went to see what held him. He was standing unhappily by a littered desk disconsolately picking at a few papers, seeds, dead leaves.

"Come," I invited him. He shrugged impatiently and refused to look at me.

"I lack the time," he growled. Ho-ho, so I had called his bluff, and found it as empty as some of his open cages.

"So, Père Pinchon," I said derisively, relishing the moment, "it seems you never have the time for anything worth while. Or perhaps you are ashamed? You don't want to expose your shame to public view?"

He was silent, he would not come. Perhaps he was making plans against me, but deciding first to put his zoo in order. One might hope so. Yes, I felt sure he was not a bad man; weak, perhaps, or thoughtless, needing to be bearded now and then.

Laughing at his discomfort, I left the room and went away, back to the city. Pappi was home, and let me use a typewriter. I made out a press release, handed it to the editor of a bi-weekly called l'Information, and wondered what would happen when police and Père Pinchon read the paper in the morning.

The denouement of the affair came rapidly enough.

Early the following morning I went down into the street, and made my way through the city towards the hotel. I would claim my sack of goods, pay the rent, change into my other shirt and disappear from the sight of gendarmes and zoo authorities. No purpose could be accomplished by throwing myself at the law, nothing could be gained by being captured.

En route to the hotel I purchased a copy of l'Information, and there in the centre of the front page was the story: Au Zoo du Fort St Louis.

UN HOMME OUVRE DES CAGES ET LAISSE S'ENFUIR DES ANI-
MAUX.

Well, perhaps it would do some good, one could only hope
so. In a few days or a week the police would forget the matter in
the face of more pressing affairs, and then the pleasure of the
city would be mine once more.

The hotel itself was hard by the Quartier Bouillé, a high-
walled compound tenanted by the military and police, but the
hour was still early and none were in the street near at hand. In
fifteen minutes' time they could come and search in vain. *Patron*
was sweeping the bar-room as I entered, and started in alarm
when he saw me. He paused to pass one hand across his glabrous
dome, his Adam's apple joggling up and down, and consternation bulged his eyes like those of a trodden toad.

"Monsieur," he pleaded. "Monsieur."

Two figures arose from chairs near by. Ten thousand demons
the police! So early? They waited already? Sudden beads of
sweat pricked my scalp, a clamour for quick flight or violent
action roused my blood. Could I turn and run? But they were too
close! God, who would have thought ...

"Monsieur," said one curtly, "your papers, please."

Papers? So it had begun, it always began thus. But my
passport was back in the apartment.

"Uh, I don't have them with me." I hedged. "May I be of
service to you in any way?"

"You are Australian, yes?" the officer queried. His *confrère*
had moved to prevent me from darting through the door. Well,
it had happened, Pinchon had reported me and they had probably
waited all night. I was caught.

"Yes, I am."

Patron continued to goggle. What use was there in concealing
facts? I could not regret what I had done. Lies would not only be
futile, but would cast an ardour of shame on a worthy act.

"And will you inform us of your activities during the night
before last?"

Why not? They would find out.

"I was busy with affairs in the zoo," I stated.

The officer blinked his surprise, and exchanged a significant
glance with his companion.

"You opened the cages? You are the man who let the animals free?"

"But of course, monsieur. Who else?"

Such naive candour disturbed the logical trend of his inquisition, and for a moment he seemed uncertain what to say. Obviously there was no point in seizing and handcuffing this fool. He was offering no resistance.

"You are aware, of course, that this is forbidden?"

"Forbidden, monsieur?" I feigned surprise. "But forbidden by whom?"

"By law. By the police."

"Liberating suffering animals is certainly not forbidden by *le bon Dieu*, monsieur. And I believe His authority is still in advance of yours. The torture of animals is surely wrong; how then can the release of tortured animals be equally wrong?"

He studied me carefully for a moment, possibly wondering if I was some obscure form of evangelist come to deliver the animal kingdom from the thrall of mankind. Then he indicated the door.

"You will come with us. I must advise you not to offer any resistance."

They took me to the *gendarmerie* hard by the prison in Rue Amiral de Gueydon, and a morning of intermittent interrogation commenced. The usual questions were asked and repeated in various guises designed to trick the truth from the mouths of liars, and at one point I was escorted to Felix's apartment to retrieve my passport.

The morning was confined within a small, bare whitewashed room with nothing but several chairs and a single desk. Two officers took turns at the questioning, and then I was left alone without lunch; there had been no breakfast either. I was briefly interrogated by a stout middle-aged major, who appeared vaguely amused to be in the presence of such a quaintly afflicted foreigner; but tempers grew short as the hours grew long. To the most frequent query, "Why did you free the animals?" I would finally only reply "Because there was no one else to do it", and this seemed to confuse them. But confusion exploded about us in shouts and excited abuse when, having laboriously typed out a twisted confession for me to sign, they handed it to me and I tore it up without bothering to read it.

A conference was held beyond my hearing.

"Monsieur!"

An officer came to the door and observed me coldly.

"It has been decided that your presence is not required on Martinique. You will, therefore, be deported."

Deported? The word burst through my brain like a pistol-shot. Deported to where? No, impossible!

"But look," I protested, "it's only —"

"We have been in contact with your consul. You have a certain amount of money, which will be used for your transportation. There is a ship in two days' time. You will remain in custody until that time."

A ship to where? Dominica? Barbados? One of the British islands? I would slip away from the ship before it sailed. I would come back, somehow. On a native sloop, I'd pay them to land me secretly.

"Where to?" I asked angrily.

"As far as possible, towards Australia. To the Pacific at least, away from the Caribbean. It has been agreed that you may find your peculiar talents of more service to you in your native Oceania."

TAHITI

In the third-class lounge of the *Tahitien* I sat with Marge and Patsy, sharing a bottle of perfume with a vacant-eyed vahiné called Annette. Better to sit with friends, it seemed, than wander about the decks where officers and stewards were seeking those who should already be ashore.

"Heavens, I don't know how you can do it," Patsy said, and shuddered. "It tastes like … like stale embalming fluid, or something."

It was doubtful if Annette had been able to taste anything for the last hour. She had ignored the warning bell, and announcements on the broadcast system, and refused to go ashore.

If any officials questioned us, I felt, their attentions would instantly centre themselves on her.

"Don't drink it all," Marge pleaded. "I thought it'd last me a year. Please?"

It was half a litre of Tiare Tahiti in an ornamental bottle, but little more than a quarter now remained. The two girls had been surprised to learn I was travelling on the *Tahitien* after all, but I explained I had taken advantage of a last-minute cancellation, and bought a ticket.

Tears began to roll down Annette's cheeks. With unsteady deliberation she lifted a garland of frangipani from her neck and placed it around Patsy's, then broke off one of the flowers and tucked it behind Marge's left ear.

"Oh, isn't she a darling?" Patsy cried, and kissed her affectionately. "We're going to miss you, Annette. But honey, you'd better go. Or you'll end up in Australia."

Perhaps I should leave and join the throng on deck, I reflected. It might be better to move around, rather than linger for long in one place. There were not many others in the lounge. At all events I must not be caught until well clear of port, or I might be transferred to an island vessel bound for Papeete. I had come aboard at midday, armed with a visitor's permit such as was freely given on request at the Messageries Maritimes office down near Vaima's; Cliff and Denny had brought my few belongings on board with their own, and since then I had quietly manoeuvred in such fashion as to avoid the attentions of immigration officials, ship's officers, visiting police and a host of inquisitive stewards in quest of tips.

At two o'clock the gangway was closed to any further visitors, and passengers who came aboard were obliged to show their tickets. At four o'clock all remaining visitors were urged to leave the ship, instructions to leave at once were broadcast repeatedly, the warning bell sounded and officials commenced a casual check of those who remained on board.

Annette twined both arms around my neck and damply kissed me, then buried her face at my neck and shook with gentle sobs, occasionally pausing to sniffle and wipe her nose on my shirt.

"Poor darling," said Patsy. "We'd better get her ashore, before they take the gang-plank up. Oh no, look who's coming!"

An American called Ralph was hurrying towards us, mildly distraught; he was a strange individual of perhaps thirty-five, tall and swarthy and loose-limbed, whose supercilious insolence estranged both men and women and whose air of disciplined dissolution suggested some sinister secret vice. Two ship's officers and a steward had entered the lounge in his wake.

"Where's Cliff and Denny?" he demanded when he saw us. "Immigration want to see them in the first-class lounge. Can't find them anywhere on the ship."

The two officers watched Annette as I disentangled myself, and issued some instruction to the steward.

"On deck," I said. It would be wise to leave the lounge at once. "I'll tell them; I know where they are."

The steward came to Annette, urging her to leave, and I rose.

"Monsieur? Your name, if you please?" One of the officers held a sheaf of lists in his hand.

My name? Quickly, what name? Well, I had known this would happen, one would have to take the chance. Moving closer to him, hoping that neither Ralph nor the girls would overhear my answer, I said, "Rause. Dan Rause. American, destination Sydney, fourth class."

He perused the fourth-class list.

"Ah yes, thank you."

He turned to Annette, who was sobbing in the arms of the patient steward, and I fled on deck to find Denny and Cliff. It evolved that small formalities were required concerning the export of their motor-bikes from the island.

Soon the gang-plank was raised, lines cast off, and amid an intense confusion of anxious farewells the *Tahitien* moved away from Commerce Quay. Papeete fell behind as we turned into the channel leading out to sea through the reefs: and the thrill of the lonely challenge coursed through my blood, feeding on the triumph of the moment. The vessel throbbed with steady power, passengers were walking the decks and gathering in saloons, or clustering at vantage points to gaze back at Papeete, and the purple mountains stroked with sunset, stoking their hearts with memories and regrets. I had wanted to stay for ever on Tahiti, and in a sense I would; I would never leave, the police would hold my name in a special "Illegally Missing" file, and wonder where I hid.

Nine days, then, to the first port of call at Vila in the New Hebrides, and another couple of days to Noumea. Among four hundred passengers I was a solitary fugitive, riding the tide of circumstance, exposed to the sensitive antennae of professionals accustomed to detecting stowaways. Aye, but I had the advantage: the advantage of being only one hidden among these hundreds, and of having good companions who would warn me of any harm, and watch my cause.

The bell for supper rang, and I took counsel with my friends.

"You going in?" Denny asked curiously.

"Yes. Best to act like everyone else. If they kept noticing me around and never saw me at meals, they'd soon figure out what was going on."

"First night. There could be some sort of check."

"Denny and I could go to the first sitting," Cliff suggested, "and see what happens."

"Good trick."

There would be three sittings in fourth class, and those who arrived in the saloon first would be the first served. Two long ranks of tables end to end ranged the centre of the hall, with ledges fixed against three walls where others ate; serving counters occupied one end and three stewards served. Cliff and Denny would attend the first sitting and report on any hazards I might face.

I occupied myself with small affairs, and after they had eaten they met me up on deck.

"Nothing," they said. "No check. Confusion all over the place, anyone sitting anywhere, and the stewards half pissed. Potage, cold cuts, and pineapple with condensed milk."

I chose a position in full view at a central table, and since no one of the fifty who sat at this sitting was aware of anything untoward, there were no whispered jests or sly smiles for the stewards to intercept.

Fourth-class passengers were distributed in perhaps a dozen cabins, each with eight bunks, and in dormitories forward in Number One hold: and, since I had not been allotted any bunk, I cast about and decided to claim one of several vacant bunks at a lower level in the hold, where ten soldiers en route to Noumea had established themselves. It seemed likely that inquiring stewards might not bother to come here, thinking only soldiers occupied that level: but if they did I would be trapped in a cul-de-sac, and would have to parry their questions as best I could. In order to minimise this risk, I selected two companions whom I trusted, who occupied berths of strategic value, and to them I confided my condition. One was Lance, who occupied Cabin 301 to starboard and who would be one of the first aware of any organised search of official check; the second was David, who occupied Cabin 304 in a similar position by the port corridor.

Certain signals would advise me of any form of crisis or alarm. Cliff and Denny, up above me, would provide a second line of defence against unheralded intrusion by officials.

On the first day out from Tahiti a pattern of events suggested early discovery of the vessel's uninvited guest. As I was leaving breakfast, which was more or less continuous with passengers arriving as others left the room, the portly first steward in charge of fourth-class welfare chose to address me just outside the door.

"Have you eaten well, monsieur?" he asked politely.

"Thank you, yes."

Why had he elected to accost me, in particular? Or had he addressed others in this fashion? He scrutinised my face with professional interest … or was it professional suspicion?

"Your name, monsieur?" he blandly inquired.

A little bubble of panic grew in my stomach. He knew, he knew! Why else should he be lurking there, waiting to ask my name? He had certainly not challenged either Cliff or Denny, who had eaten earlier, or they would have told me.

"Denny Clarke," I said levelly.

"Clarke," he mused. "And of what nationality?"

"Canadian."

"Then you speak some French, no?"

"No, monsieur."

"Ah. And the food, it is all right?"

Why, he was merely concerned about the food. On the *Cale-*

donien there had been near mutiny in fourth class when we accused the stewards, who belonged to a catering firm contracting to the shipping line, of pocketing funds which should have been used to buy fresh food at Panama. The captain had intervened, and meals improved at once.

So I shrugged and said resignedly, "It is food. I suppose it's adequate, for fourth class."

He patted my shoulder. "*D'accord*, monsieur. If I can be of any service ..."

Later in the morning I was informed by a scout that everyone was being issued with certain forms to complete, landing *fiches* which demanded passport details and points of destination.

"Your *fiche*, monsieur?" demanded a steward with a thin and wolfish face. His manner was as suavely brusque as his pencil moustache.

"You've got it already," I said, preparing to move on.

"I have it?" He glanced at me skeptically. "Your name, please?"

"Cliff Rich." Cliff had already handed his in. Surely this starved little mountebank would not connect faces with their names so early in the voyage?

"Ah, Rich. Yes, I have it. You are one of those with the big motor-bikes, is it not?"

"That's right." Again I moved to pass on. Damn him, I wanted no truck with stewards. They might happen to discuss me and discover I had several names.

"So powerful, eh?" he purred happily.

"Yes. Excuse me," I said, smiling agreeably, and strode off.

And yet a third time there came another steward who caught me just as I emerged on deck. The system of warning was not functioning as well as I had hoped. He carried the inevitable list in his hand.

"Have you been issued with linen, monsieur?" he asked.

"Thanks, yes." Linen had been issued the previous evening. I could hear one of the girls calling to me from the deck above.

"Pete! Oh, Pete! Here's that Stanley Gardner story."

Damn her, I could only ignore her cries.

The steward seemed doubtful. "But I don't think so, monsieur. Do I have your signature?"

"Hey, Pete, you deaf?"

"Everyone has my signature. I've done nothing but fill out papers and *fiches* ever since I came aboard."

David moved down the well-deck to intercept and hold the girl's attention. Bless David, then!

"But your name is …"

Devil with his questions. Well, I would toss another onion in the broth.

"Lance Marsden."

"Marsden? But I don't … ah yes. Cabin 301. Very well, monsieur."

During that afternoon there was the matter of lifeboat drill. All those who had boarded at Tahiti were commanded, over the broadcast system, to don their lifebelts and assemble on the boatdeck. Should I go? Certainly I would not be missed, if I did not. Would they check off names on a list? And I had no lifebelt, I would have to find one. Aye, but perhaps it was better to be bold. A watchful steward might chance to miss me, or note that I failed to attend, and question me: and the more I was seen in public affairs, walking freely and without fear, the less likely I would be to attract suspicion. If I could last three days without being caught, I would probably be safe for as long as I chose to stay aboard.

I stole a jacket from the dormitory and followed the others to the boatdeck; persons from all classes were there. No one bothered to check any names. An officer briefly lectured us first in French and then in English, and we were dismissed. In our absence stewards had been searching out new passengers who neglected to attend the parade.

Twice during the day there were casual inspections of our quarters by officers, but each time I was warned and moved elsewhere. But at nine o'clock that night, when most of us were abed, someone rapped twice and twice again on the steel deck just above my head.

The second-phase alarm! Some form of inspection was in progress, and they were too close for me to mount two flights of stairs and escape on deck.

The soldiers near me appeared to be asleep, rocked by the easy roll of the ship and shushed by the rush of spray swishing past the hull outside from the cleaving bows. The hold was in darkness, dimly lit by lights from the upper level where Cliff and Denny were. A large tarpaulin used to cover the hatch in port was in one corner of the hold, roped in a neat roll: it was the only possible refuge which could hide me. Seizing my blanket and clothes and sandals, I darted over to the bundle and unlashed it; earlier I had assured myself that this could be easily done. A torch flashed at the head of the stairs, and the legs of two officers appeared as they began to descend.

Horns of Satan, but the warning had come late! They must have been asleep upstairs when the officers appeared, and given the signal under their very noses. Hastily I unrolled the heavy canvas, drew it back over me, and doubled up in a ball with my clothes and blanket hugged against me as the officers gained the floor of the hold. From one side I could see the light of torches flash to and fro.

"Poilus," said one. "Only soldiers."

"Have them sweep it out in the morning," said the other. "Phew, smells like a sack of oysters."

Once the beam of a torch played full on the canvas under which I lay, but the many layered fold was too stiff to suggest a body underneath and a moment later the officers went away.

For a time I lay there, in case any of the soldiers had now woken, but after twenty minutes crept back to my bunk. Thereafter I only entered the hold when the soldiers were asleep, and left before they woke in the morning, leaving nothing to suggest that anyone had been present.

"Where do you sleep?" Ralph asked on the second day. We were sitting on the forward hatch watching David and a French girl play dominoes. His tone held a note of confidential inquiry, and his beautiful, soft eyes were steadily fixed on mine. For reasons of his own he must have noted that I seemed to have no berth in any of the men's cabins or dormitories.

"On deck," I said briefly. Abroad on deck at night one stumbled over couples in odd corners, wrapped in blankets.

"Where?" he persisted. But why would he wish to know?

"What's it to you?"

He shrugged, but still regarded me with an interested yet disdainful stare.

"One of the stewards wanted to know," he said. "He was asking, earlier."

Indeed. There seemed to be more stewards than enough for the hundred and fifty fourth-class folk; and since there were less than twenty of us whose native tongue was English, we comprised a small minority which stood out from the rest. If stewards began breathing down my neck, I might have to disappear altogether, and hide myself in some crevice like a rat.

"Give him my compliments," I said irritably, "and tell him to go to hell, that I sleep on deck with a woman."

"Oh." He seemed to be disappointed. "Which one?"

Stab me softly, but he should have a list in his hand and a pencil to make notes. He would make a good steward.

"The one with the square navel. Get lost."

I rose and went amidships to the third-class quarters, and found Marge and Patsy in their cabin with an English girl. I had already noted the location of their berth as an adequate source of temporary refuge, if I found myself in flight through the ship; they would help me with no hesitation, I knew, if I revealed the need.

"Deputation," I announced. "The boys appointed me to invite you lovely people to their humble fourth-class rabbit warren. Come and sunbake on the peak."

"Who's there?" asked Marge thoughtfully.

"Oh, everyone of importance, everyone who loves you. Mike and Lance, Denny and Cliff, Rause and —"

"We'll come," Patsy announced, sparkling with a smile. "The Austrian's not there, is he?"

"No."

No one loved the Austrian. Every time he saw a man and girl strolling the deck hand in hand he would spit, or laugh maliciously, or mutter salacious comments which could barely be overheard. Women avoided him and melted away from his approach; men regarded him with uneasy distaste.

The three girls came with me to lie in the sun on blankets, on the forecastle; if I was supposed to be sleeping on deck with a woman, I decided, it would be wise to be seen in the company of women during the day. Besides, there was a pleasing irony in lying with them in the sun, engaging in mild flirtation and lazy conversation, while officers on the bridge gazed towards us with derisive envy and binoculars.

The hare was eating lettuce in the middle of the field, but the hounds were still upwind and unaware.

One day, when I lay on Denny's bunk reading a borrowed novel, I noticed the Austrian near by in company with his only friend, a pale Swiss lad who mistook obscene manners for a worldly attitude of savoir-faire. They were standing a few yards away, engaged in tricking money from a puzzled, young French soldier of perhaps eighteen years. I had met the Austrian in Papeete, lecherously admiring pornographic pictures he had purchased, and he had spoken of the illustrated sex-books he had bought. His brain was a breeding-ground for psychotic purulence, and the handiwork of perverts was secreted in his luggage: he was travelling to Sydney and planned to sell it there.

Several times I had seen him tricking the guileless with three coins, playing a version of heads and tails which he described as crown and boot. The game was played by three men. Each would spin a coin in the air simultaneously, catch it, and at once slap it down on his wrist for all to see. If three heads showed, or three tails, the coins were tossed again. Usually the coins would fall showing two of a kind, and one odd face: and the man with the odd coin won.

The Austrian and the Swiss cheated in such fashion that no stranger could ever win. They "butterflied" their coins, so that they only appeared to spin; and if the Austrian showed a head, the Swiss would show a tail. No matter what side the third man showed his coin would make a pair with one of the others; and the man with the odd coin, the Austrian or the Swiss, would inevitably win.

When on promenade with the girls I had overheard the Austrian making indecent comments, but any open conflict on deck would have caused the girls embarrassment and brought undue attention to myself. Now the time seemed opportune; most folk were up on deck.

Discarding the book, I rose, and yawned, and pretended interest in the game. They let the soldier win once, and then he began to lose again.

"What do you call it?" I inquired.

"Crown and boot," said the Austrian. He threw me a speculative glance, but seemed to decide against an invitation.

"How is it played?"

He explained the principle, and added, "You've never seen it before?"

"No." It must have been one of the commonest games in taverns throughout the world.

"Well, you like to play?"

"Oh, I don't know. I never gamble for francs, you can't buy anything with them. Besides, I'm not lucky."

"What you mean? What do you gamble for?"

"American money. Or Australian. But I'm not much of a gambler."

But the mention of dollars and pounds whetted his appetite, for francs would be useless in Australia.

"You got dollars? You want to gamble?"

"Oh, I've got dollars."

A cunning light entered his eyes, and he shrugged as if with sad reluctance.

"Well, all right, if you want." He handed me the Frenchman's coin. "But only once or twice, this isn't my lucky day. How much you want to spin for?"

I pretended to hesitate, then took money from my pocket and counted it in front of him. There were fifteen dollars I had purchased from a tourist in Papeete, the remainder was six dollars worth of francs.

"That's all I've got," I said "Twenty-one dollars' worth."

"Hey? But you want to throw for all that?" He licked his lip and gave me a strained regard.

"Might as well." I grinned. "Treble or nothing. One throw."

The Swiss fidgeted nervously, and exchanged an anxious glance with his colleague.

"All right," said the Austrian. "All right then."

I placed the money on the deck under the toe of my sandal,

and each of them placed francs to the same value in front of them.

"Ready?"

We all tossed. But even as they moved to catch their coins I pushed the Swiss lad in the chest, and drove my fist against the Austrian's mouth. The Swiss stumbled against the companionway, the Austrian reeled back and fell against the framework of tiered bunks. Rapidly I scooped the three piles of currency from the floor, and stowed them in my pocket.

"Bastard!" cried the Austrian, wiping a plump hand across his mouth. "Bastard, you steal!" He scrambled to his feet, glaring wildly, and flung himself forward, head down and flailing his fists. An easy target. Again my fist crashed against his mouth, so that his head snapped back and he slowly crumpled to the floor. The Swiss lad was staring in horror, gripping the rails of the companionway and with one foot already on the lower step, as if prepared to flee; but I only glanced at him once, and then ignored him. Three male passengers near by, Frenchmen, chattered among themselves with excited inquiry.

The Austrian pushed himself to a sitting position, fumbling at his mouth with one hand.

"*Verfluchter Dreck!*" he cursed thickly. "*Hat mir die Zähne kaputt geschlagen!* Ah-h-h . . ."

"But ... but why?" asked the young French soldier, gazing at me as if I might be mad.

"Because he cheated. And because he's no good anyway."

"Cheated?"

"Yes." I nudged the Austrian with my toe. "Isn't that so?"

But he was silent, spitting into his hand, and I nudged him in the ribs with some force.

"Tell him you cheated."

Tears were rolling down his cheeks as he glanced up, and even malice and hatred had drained from his eyes on a tide of extravagant self-pity.

"My teef!" he cried unhappily. He held out two broken teeth, capped with gold. "You break my teef. Why? Why? I do nothing to you?"

"You called a decent girl a whore the other day, when I was walking with her. And you cheated just now. Right?"

"No, I don't. Yes, yes! All right, yes I cheat." He spat blood on the deck and stared down at it inconsolably. Would he report me to the stewards? Would there be some form of inquiry? Devil, he could do me greater harm than he knew.

"Better quit cheating," I said. "And insulting people. And don't bother making trouble. Those Sydney police are tough on characters who try and smuggle in dirty photographs and books. Understand?"

He said nothing. I nudged him again.

"You understand?"

"Yes, yes, I understand. Nothing trouble."

I left him sitting there, and the Swiss had scurried ahead as I made my way on deck. As a certain officer had remarked, there was something below that smelt like a sack of oysters.

〰〰〰〰〰

"Strike me lucky, what a miserable-looking place!" David muttered, gazing ahead through mists of light rain. "Romance of the Pacific, look at it."

It was the afternoon of the ninth day, and we were clustered at the windows of an enclosed deck just below the bridge. Ahead of us the New Hebrides appeared as an olive smear of flat shadow dimly seen through veils of weeping mist.

"Not so bad, though," said Lance. He had called in there on his way to Tahiti. "You can get Foster's lager there, in Vila."

"Vahinés?" suggested Mike.

"Not that you'd notice. Melanesian types, I think. But they got Foster's."

"They reckon we lie off, out in the bay," Denny said. "Mightn't be able to get ashore anyway."

"Aw, there'll be a launch or something. We'll be there all day tomorrow. We'll get ashore somehow."

"Who wants to?" David asked. "Looks like it rains for ever around here."

Personally it was a matter of small importance whether or not I could go ashore; only four persons were aware of my position, and all the others, including stewards, seemed to assume without question that I was a passenger. I watched as a seaman made his way forward on the well-deck below, clutching flags in his hand;

he paused by the foremast, untied a line, and raised the French tricolour on the port flag-halyard. Crossing to the other side, he raised a British ensign on the starboard halyard.

"British?" I inquired. "What's that for?"

Lance was uncertain.

"Some kind of split-Government deal they have here, I think. French and British."

"You mean, part of the Hebrides is British territory?"

"Something like that. Trust territory or something."

This was interesting. Conceivably, then, it might be wise to land at Vila; the British were less hasty than the French, and inclined to easier tolerance of Australians. But of course, if half of the Hebrides was British, there would be Australians there; and, if Australian officials were sometimes the worst of all, there would surely be others of my nation one could easily approach. I now had thirty pounds, a goodly sum: certainly something or other could be arranged.

But someone tapped me on the shoulder, and when I saw a steward there a sudden gust of premonition fired my bowels.

"The chief. He wishes to speak with you."

Cliff and Denny studied me with brief anxiety, and turned away. Lance was suddenly stiff, pretending not to notice. But what could the chief steward want? He was standing not thirty feet away, waiting, obviously wishing to speak with me in confidence. It could be no routine matter; they employed no such finesse.

Why had I been singled out for the chief's attention? Fear enveloped me in bloodless wings, but I went to him, forcing discipline on tingling nerves.

"Yes?"

"Come, monsieur." We moved aside from a couple standing near us, and then he halted to survey me with a cynical regard.

"You are the one, eh? The Australian."

I would use David's name. If he thought I was Australian, I would be David Lawson.

"What's on your mind, chief?"

"Making trouble. You know it is forbidden?"

Many things were forbidden; such as travelling on French

liners, and sleeping on French bunks and eating French food, without paying.

"You are the one who hit the Austrian?"

Ah, so that was it.

"I hit him, yes."

"Why?"

"Because he has a serpent in his mouth."

"Fighting is strictly forbidden on board," he announced firmly. I was silent. His statement rested well enough by itself.

"I shall have to make a report to the chief officer," he went on, and waited. Waited for what? For me to protest, or shed tears, or offer him a bribe? A pox on him, he could make his report.

"Go ahead," I said, and shrugged. I would leave the ship at the earliest possible moment. "He deserved it. I hit him twice."

He nodded with satisfaction. "And your name?"

"David Lawson."

"Lawson?" he echoed, incredulous. "You are David Lawson?" He looked at me with a strained air of disapproval. "But no, monsieur, I do not believe so." And turning to the group by the windows he cried out, "Mister Lawson!"

David turned around and left his place to come towards us. Eyes of a buttered dog, what was happening? I was caught. I had been too clever, there was no way out of this. Or could I pretend that I had lied to try and dodge his report, and give my right name as someone else?

"Monsieur," said the chief to David, "your name is David Lawson, is it not?"

David intercepted the flicker of an eyelid.

"Er, no, chief. I'm Lance Marsden."

"Marsden? But ... *Meutre*!" He was confused. As a man who doubtless prided himself on remembering names and faces, since his position would demand it daily, he suddenly found his talent ridiculed. "But I called Lawson. You answered!"

"I thought you said Marsden. You're already talking to Dave Lawson. What's the bloody matter with you?"

"Eh? Lawson?" He fixed his eye on some distant point, twisted his mouth in a wry grimace, and gave a vast sigh. "*Eh bien*, Lawson," looking back at us.

He made a note of the name and went away shaking his head and muttering to himself. David grinned at me.

"You're on report," he said. "Or I am. Anyway David Lawson is, for flattening the Austrian."

"Proud of it. We'll play it as it goes."

I rested my hand on his shoulder, and we walked back to the others chuckling.

NEW HEBRIDES

At dusk the vessel anchored in a cove half a mile out from the town of Vila, a small Pacific outpost steeped in early twilight and shrouded by grey clouds. Passengers were permitted ashore, and Denny and Cliff led the way amidships to the gang-plank on brief reconnaissance. There were no formalities; no papers were demanded, one merely walked down the gang-plank and boarded a waiting launch. Nor were there any formalities when we landed, and Lance led us along the wet and lugubrious waterfront to the Wailéle Hotel.

The bar was crowded, so we sat about a table on the veranda with bottles of Foster's lager: David and Lance, Denny and Cliff, Patsy and Marge, and a sad, little old-young Englishman called Guidon. Australian currency was used, but dollars were more than welcome and even Pacific francs were acceptable enough. Laughter and conversation raged for an hour or more, but I sat with an air of detachment wondering if I should stay ashore, or risk continuing on *Tahitien* to Noumea.

What part of the Hebrides was governed by the British? Did British vessels call here? What would happen if I was questioned by the chief officer? I needed some source of information, a man who had his finger on the pulse of the local scene. Thoughtfully I watched the men who came and went, those who sat with others and those who sat alone: and after some time I approached a certain man, and invited him to sit with us. We were strangers, I explained, and hoped he would honour us by settling small disputes which concerned the Hebrides.

He came from Santo in the north, and his name was Bill Giles; he was a lean and weather-tanned Australian approaching forty-five years, a laconic wit and engaging raconteur. Everyone immediately liked him for his personable manner; his conversation was direct, to the point and even bold, laced with congenial humour and the flavour of far places, yet touched with a gracious restraint for the sake of Marge and Patsy.

Later, as he came back from the restroom, I found an excuse to intercept him. If he was the man I thought he was — and I had watched him closely — he was not the type to run to the gendarmes with sly reports.

"I have a problem," I began, confronting him at a distance from our table. He considered me in watchful silence. "Point one is that someone travelled from Papeete to Vila, on the *Tahitien*, without a ticket."

He accepted this with a thoughtful nod, inspecting his fingernails.

"Point two is that this person doesn't know whether it would be best to get off here, or at Noumea."

He glanced at me swiftly. "No problem there, friend," he said gravely. "You get off here."

"Why?"

"I'll tell you why." He accepted a cigarette, and a light. "A while back I heard about two Aussies who snuk on board a French ship at Sydney — the *Caledonien*, I think — and they got caught before the ship reached Noumea. The cops grabbed 'em in Noumea, and gave them six months in the chain-gang."

"In a chain-gang? Hell's fire!"

"I'd keep the hell away from Noumea," he went on. "The French cops there are mean, and they can do what they like with you. But, now, take this place," indicating the Hebrides with a flourish of his cigarette. "It's different. It's a condominium for a start, under the joint rule of France and Britain. For all practical purposes this town here, Vila, is French; but, if anyone breaks the law, they can't just grab him and slap him in jail. There's a special clause that states a Spanish judge has to be present, whenever any sentence is passed on a prisoner. And no Spanish judge has been available for about ten years now. Get the picture?"

"But that's magnificent!" Nothing could happen to me; or if it did, what could it be?

A lazy grin spread across his face. "There's two arraigned murderers walking around this town quite openly. Cripes, they wouldn't worry about a stowaway. They might deport him to Sydney, but that's about all. And then it'd be up to the Sydney cops."

Ah, then there was still that.

"Better stay," he said, smiling as he squinted at me through cigarette smoke. "Want me to arrange a room for you?"

"Here, you mean?"

"I know the management. I can get it fixed without any silly questions."

"Well, yes thanks."

He arranged that I should be given a room in the annexe, at moderate cost. I would stay ashore, and avoid undue attentions until the vessel sailed some time tomorrow night. All the clothes I possessed I had worn ashore, I had my passport and my razor and toothbrush; the blanket and typewriter were still aboard, but these were expendable items and a hindrance to fluid movement.

When my companions set out to return to the ship, I confided my plans to Denny and Cliff and stayed behind. Perhaps I would see them in Australia. That night I slept in the annexe. Early in the morning Giles flew back to Santo, and I did not see him again.

Next day I remained a fugitive, intent on avoiding any untoward occasion which might provoke misfortune; I left the town in early morning and only returned at night, and during that night *Tahitien* sailed away. Thus, on the morning of the second day, I was the only person in town who knew who I was, or from whence I came; one could lend imagination to almost any form of story, and invent the most unlikely tales, as long as they coincided with the data in my passport: and how could anyone prove that a tale was true or false? If anyone suspected I had come aboard *Tahitien*, they had only to cable the vessel to learn that I had not. No one of that name was on their list.

"How did you arrive?" a middle-aged woman demanded. She was like some plump, half-melted candle, with tallow arms and greasy eyes.

"There are two schools of thought," I replied. "Some think I came by *Tahitien*, others say I came by way of Santos."

"But which is right?"

"Take your choice," I offered, and she arched with indignation and went away.

A plane would leave for Noumea in two days' time, making the ninety-minute flight to Noumea, and I supposed one might need some kind of visa. But if I approached the French authorities and asked for a visa now, they would have two days to think of questions and check on my replies: better, therefore, to wait until a few hours before the plane departed. With a ticket in my hand and ready to leave at once, they might more easily be tempted to rid themselves of a fool who only promised to be a nuisance.

Towards noon on the last day I presented myself at the *gendarmerie*, explaining to the receptionist that I sought a transit visa for New Caledonia.

"If you will leave your passport," she suggested, "and call again this afternoon?"

"But the plane leaves at two o'clock. See, I have my ticket."

She consulted some inner office, and I was required to present myself to a handsome, young officer within. He accepted my passports.

"A transit visa only?" he inquired. "Transit to where?"

"Through Noumea to Australia, monsieur."

He paged briefly through the first passport, found an empty page, and stamped it with a large rubber stamp.

"Three days," he said, "in Noumea." He filled in small details with a pen.

"Thank you." Well, this was too facile: rarely had I received a visa with such expeditious ease. What an intelligent, worthy, and efficient officer, a credit to his nation: he accepted me without demur, I was once again *en règle*. But then, as he was about to hand the passports back, he looked among the pages for the entry stamp to the Hebrides. He glanced through the first book twice, frowned, flicked me an inquiring glance, and began searching through the others. Whenever he found a French entry or exit stamp, or visa, he would scan it hopefully — stamps and visas for Tunisia, Dahomey, French Morocco, the Cameroons,

Algeria, French Guinea, the French Sudan, French Equatorial Africa, St Martin, and Guadeloupe and Martinique. It took some minutes.

At length he frowned thoughtfully and said, "But your entry stamp, you have none? Where did you enter the New Hebrides?"

Well, then, here it was. He would require some form of explanation, but he seemed an agreeable young blade.

"I ask your pardon, monsieur, but I don't have the faintest idea."

He leant back in his chair, rested one finger against his cheek, and regarded me with a baffled stare. He was interested rather than suspicious; obviously any *agent provocateur* would make no such admission, but would have a logical story tailored for the occasion.

"You have no idea where you entered these islands? You mean you don't remember the name of the port?"

"There was no port, monsieur. I landed on a beach."

"On a beach? What beach? Your last entry shows Tahiti. You swam here, perhaps, from Tahiti?" He was frankly astonished. One might forgive him for considering me some witless escapee from an institution.

"I was shipwrecked, more or less."

"More or less? You mean you had a yacht, a motor vessel, and you were wrecked? What was its name?"

"It was a catamaran, monsieur, a small catamaran called *Tiare Tahiti*."

"I see," he murmured vaguely, as thoughts hunted through his head like hungry rats. "A catamaran. You came from Tahiti, in a catamaran?"

"Yes."

"Alone?"

"All alone, by myself." And then added soberly, "It was a mistake."

"A mistake." He drew a hand across his mouth, smothering an urge to laugh. "You, ah, meant to go to Sydney, no doubt? But you became lost in the course of a few thousand miles by catamaran, and found yourself here instead?"

"No, no, monsieur. I mean, I'd only borrowed the boat for the day, from a friend in Papeete, but the wind was strong and blew me out to sea."

He nodded bleakly. "It blew you half-way across the Pacific Ocean to the Hebrides?"

"Yes, monsieur."

"And how long were you at sea? All night?"

I swallowed a smile. Obviously he was not one to be deceived by such nonsense. But what could he prove? Or disprove?

"Five weeks, monsieur. I was at sea five weeks."

He closed his eyes for a moment, gently massaging them with his fingertips, and then viewed me with droll mistrust.

"And of course, you carried enough food and water for a month or two. Or perhaps you slept through the voyage? Or stopped at convenient hotels?"

"It was a hard journey, many days I don't remember at all. When it rained, I had water —" thinking of the animals in the zoo — "and I lived on fish. I had fishing equipment with me. I had gone out just beyond the reefs to fish."

It was impossible to check on such a story; and just as impossible to believe it. But how could I be punished for some indiscretion which the law could only guess at, and never hope to prove?

"But, of course," he said patiently, "you managed to bring your luggage?"

"All was left behind. The only things I have are my passport, some money, and the clothes you see me wearing."

"Oh?" He was thoughtful for a moment. "At what beach did you land?"

"Somewhere north, I think. For two days I was lost in jungle, and then I found a road. The road led here."

"H'm. It is not at all possible, of course, that you travelled illegally on the *Tahitien*?"

"Monsieur?"

He tapped his finger against his jaw, studying me with interest from under lowered brows.

"No, of course not, that would be against the law."

For some moments he was silent, gazing down in meditation at the desk. It might have been pleasant, I reflected, to take him out and have a drink, and be able to laugh together at this absurd childish tale, but he belonged to the enemy camp, and there could be no compromise.

"I congratulate you," he said finally, "on your excellent health. It has not interfered with your imagination." He handed my passports to me. "I strongly recommend that you join the plane at two o'clock, without fail. And without luggage. *Bonjour*, Captain Bligh."

NEW CALEDONIA ▬▬▬▬▬

NOUMEA

The evening was yet early. Turning towards the docks, I strolled down to the harbour edge and cast speculative glances at the ships. Which of them might be found for Australian ports? That handsome Swedish freighter, perhaps: it would be good to travel again aboard a Swede. Ah, there was an Argentinian, sleek and grey, and I had never been to Argentina — but no. I had no wish to go there now. Nothing but Australia would do.

Joyful expectation raced through me. Australia — the very name was a cadence of deep music. The South Land, Terra Australis. Her name was an exclamation on the tongues of foreign folk, a word provoking quiet awe, a symbol of remote and unknown lands lying beyond the limits of the sea.

And there, why, farther along the dock was a British ship, black hull daubed with red lead and decks stained with rust, an old Liberty ship. But were there no Australian ships? And beyond the British ship, that great black liner: the *Caledonian*, perhaps, on her way back from Sydney to Marseilles? But, no, she had already returned. The *Polynèsien*, then? I walked closer. Three sister ships plied the Marseilles-Sydney run. But, no, the *Polynèsien* had a white stack, it was not the *Polynèsien*.

But … what?

It was the *Tahitien*! She was still here, but, of course, this was her last French port of call before Sydney, and one of the most important.

Ho, and all my friends would be on board? Cliff and Denny and Lance and Patsy and Marge and — but I would go aboard at once! I strode towards the gangway, joyous with delighted purpose. Hey, but this was a fine event, and I chuckled with a new exhilaration as I thought of their expressions of surprise. And what of the stewards? Why, I could snap my fingers at them now. I had never seen them before: I was a lawful person, my passport was in order, I could laugh at them and swear I had never seen them before in my life. What were they talking about?

And they must have missed me by now. They would certainly realise someone had mysteriously disappeared. What had happened when David Lawson had been summoned, following the chief steward's report, to explain his reasons for fighting the Austrian? Ha-ha, what a fine confusion there must have been, with the chief steward running around the vessel in despair, searching for me!

But wait …

I paused as I mounted the gangway to consider a new thought, and my blood surged wildly. The *Tahitien* was bound for Sydney, and I wished to go to Sydney. She could take me. I could travel on her. But with a ticket. Could I buy a ticket? I probably had enough money to buy a ticket. Sydney was not far now. Joyful gods, but what a magnificent enterprise, what splendid irony, to re-join *Tahitien* with a ticket, where everyone knew by now I had been a stowaway!

But the agency on shore was already closed, I knew.

Would it be possible, then, to purchase a ticket on board? Perhaps, if I avoided recognition until the thing was done. I was thoughtful, considering the chances, but there was only one thing to do, and that was try.

Mounting the gangway, I crossed the floodlit deck and entered the purser's office near by. A few passengers and two stewards stood in the spacious entrance foyer, but no one noticed me: and they would be first-class stewards, who had only see me rarely. The purser was engaged in conversation with a stout civilian, but glanced up from his papers as I knocked.

"Pardon, monsieur," I began, edging into the cabin out of sight of passers-by. "I have just arrived in Noumea, and came directly to the ship, your office ashore was closed." I handed him my passport, opened to show the entry stamp put there hours before. "I was hoping I might purchase a ticket on your ship to Sydney. I hope I am not too late?"

He brushed my face with a glance of normal curiosity and took my passport.

"Australien," he murmured. "Well, I suppose we can sell him a ticket, perhaps?" He looked inquiringly at the portly civilian and, addressing me, went on, "This gentleman is the agent, it depends entirely on him. We have almost completed the papers, you understand. The vessel sails early in the morning."

The agent observed me with impatience, and nodded shortly.

"Yes, yes. But there is only fourth class, nothing else. You will have to travel fourth class."

"A thousand thanks," I said gravely. "If you would be so kind. Ah, how much is the passage?"

"Twenty Australian pounds, and a few francs."

"Of course."

My heart was singing with happy triumph as I counted the money and handed it to him. God bless the luckless Austrian, he had done me a greater favour than he knew. I had sufficient and even a trifle left over. The ticket was made out and handed to me, with my passport, and my name and other details added to the inevitable list.

"You have your luggage?"

"Yes." The small brown-paper parcel in my hand.

"The fourth-class quarters are forward. Ask for the chief steward there, and show him your ticket. He will direct you to your berth."

Laughing to myself, I went down to the deck below and made my way forward. *Dieu*, but this was a happily ridiculous occasion: and I was on my way to Sydney? Why, all I had to do was sit down, and in four days or so the ship would be steaming through the Heads — lucky day. Life was a wonderful affair!

Weaving through familiar passages, I went to the galley and closets behind the fourth-class dining-hall, and the chief steward was there in company with Pencil-Moustache. Pencil-Moustache was standing at his ease drinking coffee, while the chief sat scribbling notes on a pad: P-M was the first to see me. His eyes grew wide, and with the cup an inch from his lips he froze in the attitude of one just about to sip.

"*'Soir*," I said agreeably. "Is one of you chief steward?"

The chief looked up. An expression of stupefaction slowly

assumed possession of his face, twitching small muscles. His mouth jerked open, but no words came forth. With a brave attempt to control laughter I coughed, and said again, "The chief steward? The purser said he would show me to my bunk."

I offered the ticket, placing it before him, but he ignored it.

"Sweet thunder," he cried, "what? But what are you doing here? Where did you —"

"I am a passenger, monsieur. I am travelling to Sydney. The purser said —"

"It's him!" P-M whinnied, spilling coffee. "By my own sacred mother ..."

The chief rose to his feet, pale and fleshy face drawn with excitement, moist eyes swelling in their sockets.

"Ticket? You have a ticket now? What is your name?" He matched up the ticket and scanned it. "Australian, yes, yes. Ha! No more David Lawson, eh? You disappear, someone takes your place, what happens? Hey?"

My broad grin refused to be controlled. "Don't know what you're talking about," I said agreeably. "You must be making a mistake. I've never seen your before."

"Hey? But from Tahiti? But I know, everyone knows: you travel from Tahiti on this ship. You punch the Austrian. You become six different people with six different names" — glancing anew at the ticket — "and none of them your own. Then suddenly you disappear, no one can find you. Where did —"

"You're mistaken," I said, shrugging. "I only joined the ship ten minutes ago. See!" I showed him my passport. "There is the entry stamp to New Caledonia, I've just arrived by air. Perhaps you confuse me with someone else?"

"Confuse? But —" He scrutinised me closely. Same face, same shirt, same jeans and sandals. "I know you, I talked with you, you ate at the second sitting. But where did you sleep? And no ticket at all, hey? And now you have another name, a quite different name. Sacred swine! And a ticket to Sydney. And you come here asking who is chief steward, hey? You don't know me yet?"

"Never saw you in my life. But you find some resemblance between myself and another person?"

"Resemblance?" shrilled P-M, but the chief signalled him to

silence. A worldly man, the chief was rapidly regaining his self-possession as he shuttled facts and probabilities around inside his mind to form a pattern of intelligent deduction. He perused the ticket again to verify my name and the purser's signature, and his jaws worked on some imagined morsel as he stabbed at me with a speculative gaze.

"Resemblance," he muttered. "Yes, yes one might say so." What good would it do to his reputation to admit, to higher authority, that he had permitted a stowaway to travel on the vessel under his very nose? That he had suffered the presence of an impostor at every meal, failing to detect him? And here was this assassin armed now with a valid ticket. What could be done against him, if he persisted in denials?

He handed the ticket to me. At least he would not be humbled by pretending to show me where Cabin 306 was.

"I believe," he said carefully, "that you might be able to find your own cabin. Meals are at the usual times. You may even possibly discover some of the passengers are familiar. But, please, it should not be necessary to amuse yourself by borrowing their names."

SYDNEY

Passengers formed queues in the first-class lounge. An official studied my passports with a speculative frown, examining the protective leather cover and its Moroccan title; another scrutinised my health certificate, recently brought up to date by careful use of a pen and the stamp pad impression of a brandy-bottle seal.

"How much money do you have?" someone asked, and I searched the balding strip of goatskin which served me as a wallet. It held a little money, an address in St Vincent, a Hinano beer label with a dozen signatures, a newspaper cutting from *l'Information*, a carefully preserved sample of creased, but virginal letterhead from the *Vancouver Sun*, a licence to carry a pistol in Costa Rica, and the sketch of a handshake signal employed by members of a certain well-known lodge.

"Two pounds," I said. "Three dollars, ten pesetas, one escudo, and a quetzal."

Sydney, my Sydney — home! The end of the trail, the last port, the final and finest goal of all. Gateway to Australia, Mecca of east-coast urgers, paradise of jackeroos and stockmen: the city which smiles on the quick and the strong, and pushes the weak to the wall. Her heart is of bitter honey, her brain a cash register, her magic wand is a whip of tungsten steel. Her mantle is spun from illusion and sparkles with slivers of hope; her underclothes are of cheesecloth begrimed with industrial soot and trimmed with gold. Proud, sly, corrosively plausible with leisurely zeal, she favours the man with the hottest dice, yet takes the foremost pew and prays aloud.

By all the gods that ever were, it was good to be back again!